# The Intensive Interaction Classroom Guide

This book is a practical guide to implementing the Intensive Interaction Approach in a school setting and provides essential technical support to teachers and practitioners from nursery to Post-16 who want to embed it into their classroom practice. Geared mainly towards supporting children with communication and social-communication difficulties arising from autism or learning difficulties, the principles apply equally to students of all levels of cognitive ability who struggle with social situations and emotional or sensory regulation.

*The Intensive Interaction Classroom Guide* brings together contributions from experienced teachers, teaching assistants, and headteachers who reflect on their practice and share practical tips to facilitate social-communication development within a nurturing classroom environment. Offering practical advice on curriculum and pedagogy and drawing on case studies, authors address key themes on a practical level, while grounding their discussions theoretically and methodologically.

Filled with practical advice and techniques, this book will be essential to anyone working in classroom settings with students who experience social-communication difficulties or need a nurturing approach to emotional well-being.

**Amandine Mourière** is a freelance autism and learning disability consultant and a Team Leader at the Intensive Interaction Institute.

**Pam Smith** is the autism support teacher and Intensive Interaction Coordinator at two Surrey special schools.

"Embedding Intensive Interaction at the heart of a school's educational, pastoral, and care provision should be seen as a vital element in meeting our children's special educational needs. This book offers reflective, insightful, and practically useful perspectives and resources that can significantly help in this process. Setting each individual child at the very centre of their own social and communicative development is what Intensive Interaction undoubtedly delivers; this book will help schools and teaching staff alike to more effectively meet that challenge."
— **Graham Firth, Intensive Interaction Institute Team Leader and Founding Director**

"Intensive Interaction IS communication, and this book illustrates this very clearly. In the 70s, when I started in SEN, we quickly realised behaviour modification was not right for our students. We began using music and dance, symbols and timetables, plus social stories. We also began to realise how much our students – and their families – could teach us! Maybe this was the beginning of Intensive Interaction . . . which has now been refined to the professional standard illustrated by the many contributors to this book. Importantly, it has not lost any of its spontaneity or its child-centred emphasis."
— **Ruth Buchan, former Headteacher Freemantles School**

"It has been a long time since Kellett and Nind's 'Implementing Intensive Interaction in Schools' did 'what it said on the box' and became every Intensive Interaction Coordinator's go-to reference, so it is great to see the arrival of *The Intensive Interaction Classroom Guide* which gives a range of contexts to the experiences of practitioners now using Intensive Interaction in classrooms. It contains some especially helpful and current references to EYFS, EHCPs, and Ofsted that both lone practitioners and Coordinators in schools will find reassuring and useful."
— **Dr Mark Barber, Consultant in Profound Intellectual Disability and Severe Communication Impairment in Australia**

# The Intensive Interaction Classroom Guide

Social Communication Learning and Curriculum for Children with Autism, Profound and Multiple Learning Difficulties, or Communication Difficulties

EDITED BY
AMANDINE MOURIÈRE AND PAM SMITH

LONDON AND NEW YORK

First edition published 2022
by Routledge
2 Park Square, Milton Park, Abingdon, Oxon, OX14 4RN

and by Routledge
605 Third Avenue, New York, NY 10158

*Routledge is an imprint of the Taylor & Francis Group, an informa business*

© 2022 selection and editorial matter, Amandine Mourière and Pam Smith; individual chapters, the contributors

The right of Amandine Mourière and Pam Smith to be identified as the authors of the editorial material, and of the authors for their individual chapters, has been asserted in accordance with sections 77 and 78 of the Copyright, Designs and Patents Act 1988.

All rights reserved. No part of this book may be reprinted or reproduced or utilised in any form or by any electronic, mechanical, or other means, now known or hereafter invented, including photocopying and recording, or in any information storage or retrieval system, without permission in writing from the publishers.

*Trademark notice*: Product or corporate names may be trademarks or registered trademarks, and are used only for identification and explanation without intent to infringe.

*British Library Cataloguing-in-Publication Data*
A catalogue record for this book is available from the British Library

*Library of Congress Cataloging-in-Publication Data*
Names: Mourière, Amandine editor. | Smith, Pam, 1959– editor.
Title: The intensive interaction classroom guide : social communication learning and curriculum for children with autism, profound and multiple learning difficulties, or communication difficulties / edited by Amandine Mourière and Pam Smith.
Identifiers: LCCN 2021013573 (print) | LCCN 2021013574 (ebook) | ISBN 9780367773298 (hardback) | ISBN 9780367773304 (paperback) | ISBN 9781003170839 (ebook)
Subjects: LCSH: Interaction analysis in education. | Social interaction in children. | Communicative disorders in children—Treatment.
Classification: LCC LB1034 .I56 2022 (print) | LCC LB1034 (ebook) | DDC 371.102/2—dc23
LC record available at https://lccn.loc.gov/2021013573
LC ebook record available at https://lccn.loc.gov/2021013574

ISBN: 978-0-367-77329-8 (hbk)
ISBN: 978-0-367-77330-4 (pbk)
ISBN: 978-1-003-17083-9 (ebk)

DOI: 10.4324/9781003170839

Typeset in Antitled
by Apex CoVantage, LLC

This book is dedicated to the amazing students with whom we share magical, soul-to-soul, Intensive Interaction moments, their families and our colleagues who work tirelessly to establish Intensive Interaction in Education. Above all to our families for their unending love and support – Nikki, Kevin, Robin & Mike.

# Contents

List of figures and tables ............................................. viii

List of contributors ................................................... ix

Foreword ............................................................. xi
*Dave Hewett*

1 Introduction ........................................................ 1
*Amandine Mourière and Pam Smith*

2 The story of Intensive Interaction ................................... 4
*Dave Hewett*

3 What do students with autism and learning disabilities need to learn? ... 15
*Pam Smith*

4 Intensive Interaction as a teaching and learning approach ............ 29
*Amandine Mourière*

5 My journey to Intensive Interaction in the Early Years Foundation Stage ... 42
*Rhianne Richards*

6 Developing a whole-school approach to using Intensive Interaction to promote social communication and well-being ............................. 52
*Debbie Stagg*

7 Intensive Interaction within the general communication curriculum .... 63
*Lana Bond and Inga K. Serafin*

8 Intensive Interaction within our holistic and child-centred approach at Brøndagerskolen ... 73
*Sanne Laudrup and Pernille Hasseriis Noach*

9 Developing the Fundamentals of Communication through free-flow play ... 86
*Julie Cassidy and Katy Snell*

10 Intensive Interaction and the birth of process-central curriculum access ... 100
*Sue Lowry and Bec Anderson*

11 Touch: the cement that binds us .................................... 114
*Julia Barnes*

12 Management issues: ensuring a school is Intensive Interaction friendly ... 126
*Anne Adams*

13 Ensuring access to Intensive Interaction through Education, Health and Care Plans ... 139
*Lucy Hankin*

14 Getting it right with recording Intensive Interaction ............... 151
*Ian Harris and Pam Smith*

Appendix 1: Video observation sheet .................................. 161

Appendix 2: Summary of observations .................................. 162

Appendix 3: A value charter for schools .............................. 163

Appendix 4: Intensive Interaction: new development form .............. 165

Appendix 5: Style/technique list ..................................... 166

Glossary ............................................................. 168

Index ................................................................ 170

# Figures and tables

## Figures

| | | |
|---|---|---|
| 3.1 | The Communication Tree (Hewett, 2018, p. 84) | 19 |
| 4.1 | The 'spiral' of progress and development | 37 |
| 5.1 | The progress track | 50 |
| 8.1 | Photo – student engaged in Intensive Interaction with an adult | 79 |
| 9.1 | Case study: Judah – progress in the Fundamentals of Communication and techniques used | 93 |
| 9.2 | Case study: Tanzeela – progress in the Fundamentals of Communication and techniques used | 96 |
| 10.1 | Magic carpet | 101 |
| 10.2 | 1–5–3 sub-structure of process-central curriculum access | 106 |

## Tables

| | | |
|---|---|---|
| 5.1 | Intensive Interaction Recording Sheet | 49 |
| 13.1 | Examples of wordings for EHC Plan, Sections A, B, E, and F | 145 |
| 13.2 | Detail of a structure to support professionals to include Intensive Interaction in EHC Plans | 148 |

# Contributors

**Anne Adams** is Head of Service at Options Higford (an Independent School and Children's Home for young people with Autism and Complex Needs) in Shropshire. She is also an Intensive Interaction Coordinator and a Director of the Intensive Interaction Institute.

**Bec Anderson** is a special needs classroom teacher and Intensive Interaction practitioner in Australia.

**Julia Barnes** is a teacher and Sensory Manager at Ravenscliffe High School, Halifax and studying on the educational doctorate course, part time, at The University of Birmingham.

**Lana Bond** is a special needs teacher and Intensive Interaction Coordinator at Woodlands School in Edgware in London.

**Julie Cassidy** is a special needs teacher and leader of curriculum and approaches in the SLD/ PMLD department at Mandeville Special School in London.

**Lucy Hankin** is a teaching assistant and Intensive Interaction Coordinator for a special school at Tettenhall Wood School in the West Midlands.

**Ian Harris** is a retired Head of Learning Support at a Further Education College and current IT consultant.

**Pernille Hasseriis Noach** is a teacher and Intensive Interaction Coordinator at Brøndagerskolen in Denmark.

**Dave Hewett** OBE led the team which developed Intensive Interaction in the 1980s and is the Honorary Life President of the Intensive Interaction Institute.

**Sanne Laudrup** is a pedagogue and Intensive Interaction Coordinator at Brøndagerskolen in Denmark.

**Sue Lowry** is a special needs teacher and Intensive Interaction Coordinator in Australia.

**Amandine Mourière** is an autism and learning disabilities consultant and a Team Leader at the Intensive Interaction Institute.

**Rhianne Richards** is an Early Years teacher and SENDCo at South Acton Nursery School & Children's Centre in London.

# Contributors

**Inga K. Serafin** is a classroom teacher and a PMLD department leader at Woodlands School in Edgware in London.

**Pam Smith** is the autism support teacher and Intensive Interaction Coordinator at Manor Mead and Walton Leigh Schools in Surrey.

**Katy Snell** trained and worked as an SLD, PMLD, and autism teacher. She is now a freelance consultant with particular interest in play, outdoor learning, and physical development.

**Debbie Stagg** is the Intensive Interaction Coordinator, a sleep practitioner, and a member of the well-being team at Freemantles School in Surrey.

# Foreword

A warm welcome to all of you hard-working, committed, earnest, loving educators who have the wisdom to suspect, or know, that introducing Intensive Interaction to your learning environment makes a huge difference for young people who potentially have the greatest learning needs. It is my privilege to introduce you to this latest volume of authoritative insights on Intensive Interaction and to recommend it to you wholeheartedly.

At the time of writing, February 2021, our society is in a dark period of great COVID-19 adversity. I am keenly aware that so many of you out there in the education environment are experiencing huge and daunting challenges. I know that most of you will be tired and stressed, probably simply focused on maintaining the core of what your workplace offers. However, it will be many months before this book is finally published. There is every prospect that by that time, as you read this, we will be in a different situation of greater ease and optimism.

With this book Amandine Mourière and Pam Smith bring you an edited volume that is something of a departure for published work from the Intensive Interaction Institute. Until now, our tradition has mainly been books giving generic advice to practitioners of all disciplines – school, college, adult services, therapists, and so on. We have tried to make our work accessible to parents and families too. However, this book recognises that the introduction of Intensive Interaction into classrooms can face a range of specific, technical, practical, and even bureaucratic complexities that might not so much apply in other disciplines. We are aware, from long experience with special educators, that these complexities might in some cases even operate as barriers to the introduction of this simple, vital, Intensive Interaction teaching and learning. We also know from experience that none of these complexities are actually barriers. Therefore, Mourière and Smith bring you the benefit of their experience in schools, fulsomely laid out.

Here you will find plenty of advice which addresses the most central of such issues. Namely, Intensive Interaction is and always has been, different. It is different from nearly all of the established, conventional teaching and learning traditions in special education over the last 40 years. The pedagogy, the teaching technique, is different. It is process-orientated rather than objectives-based. Indeed, although the expected learning outcomes are clear, the reliance on setting pre-determined goals and objectives that is ingrained into our system is not necessary. Indeed, operating aims and setting goals – these are likely to be a hindrance to the teaching and learning process. Furthermore, as you will read in detail within, this way of working – Intensive Interaction – is seen within an overall focus on the developmental reality of the learner and the recognition that early-learning type activities are, for most of the learners, the daily educational ecology which best serves them. As described herein, Intensive Interaction should and does fit easily into the cruciality of early years' work. Perhaps we should also consider whether something of this early years' work can fit into classrooms for older pupils?

## Foreword

So, I believe this volume offers a positive, supportive recognition on another aspect of this challenge. Many schools may have historically adopted a way of working into which Intensive Interaction might not easily 'fit'. This may, of course, especially be the case if the learner is within a mainstream environment. Therefore, it becomes clear that the introduction of Intensive Interaction will bring with it the necessity for some cultural change, or at least adjustment. I offer to you the view that you will find extensive advice and support on these matters within this book's variously authored chapters. School management teams will find such advice too, focusing knowledgeably on this perspective.

From the opening chapter describing something of the development of Intensive Interaction, then throughout, you will find watchwords and phrases something along the lines of collaboration, teamwork, flexibility, openness, reflection, focus on the learner, and developmental reality. These are not words of frilly optimism for the educational environment. They are down to earth concepts for the reality of Intensive Interaction's development and implementation. Successfully adopting Intensive Interaction means successfully adopting the reality of these words and phrases and the benefits they bring for everything and everybody within your learning environment.

I know and have worked with nearly all the contributors to this book, either as long-term colleagues, such as Amandine Mourière, or as members of our long-term Intensive Interaction Coordinator course, such as Pam Smith. I have been fortunate and privileged to work alongside the contributors from other countries, in their countries. I feel qualified to guarantee to you that you are receiving here the best and most authoritative Intensive Interaction classroom guide possible. Intensive Interaction profoundly and positively changes people's lives. There are young people in need out there who have yet to have their lives changed through the classroom adoption of Intensive Interaction. Please address this. I wish you, your colleagues, and your learners nothing but success and joy in your work.

**Dave Hewett**
Malvern
February 2021

# 1. Introduction

*Amandine Mourière and Pam Smith*

It is now over 15 years since a book on implementing Intensive Interaction in schools was published (Kellet and Nind, 2003), and since then a lot has happened in the world of education! The importance of children's mental health and wellbeing has come to the fore and, since September 2020, has been recognised as core within teachers' safeguarding responsibilities. Relational, play-based approaches and child-centred learning have become the focus for supporting children's learning and behaviour, replacing more behaviourist philosophies. Intensive Interaction enables learners to access emotional learning and social communication learning. It is not a prescriptive approach though; it does not work as a series of prescribed steps one follows to achieve a wanted goal or target. Instead, Intensive Interaction is a process-central approach, which means that style and techniques drive practice rather than targets and objectives. In a sense, with Intensive Interaction we embrace a whole philosophy in which the child is at the very core, valued and respected.

The idea for this book was born from feedback from professionals in education, who consistently express their struggle in getting Intensive Interaction to be recognised and supported as a substantive and established teaching approach. Whilst many teachers find the approach pertinent to their learners, they often struggle to implement it fully within their classroom settings. This is often due to the mistaken perception of Intensive Interaction as an 'optional extra', done during free time or squeezed in between 'proper' lessons rather than taking its rightful place as the curricular engine which drives all other learning.

Intensive Interaction is beautifully simple, but sadly it is too often assumed that staff can simply get on with it. This couldn't be further from the actual truth! Achieving good practice is a process which involves ongoing training, sound understanding of child and social communication development, emotional intelligence, fantastic organisational skills, and the ability to operate as a reflective practitioner to increase awareness and appreciation of Intensive Interaction techniques.

With this book we wanted to bring together contributors who have a deep appreciation of the complex simplicity of Intensive Interaction, and we individually hand-picked them to share their knowledge and offer practical advice on implementing Intensive Interaction within a school or individual classroom. Contributions included by teachers from Denmark and Australia, illustrate that whilst learning priorities for children with social communication difficulties remain the same, challenges around implementing Intensive Interaction may vary according to educational context and culture.

Delivering this book has been such an exciting project and one which has made us feel both humbled and privileged to share in the chapter authors' work. It is worth bearing in mind that these contributors have written their incredible chapters while continuing to work at the 'coal face' – teaching during the day with all

DOI: 10.4324/9781003170839-1

the additional pressures upon them, some dealing personally with the impact of COVID-19 upon themselves and their families, whilst managing to write in their spare time! They are owed a huge debt of thanks for doing this against all odds. To find the energy to do so shows just how vital they feel Intensive Interaction is to their students and their classrooms.

As described by Dr Dave Hewett in Chapter 2, Intensive Interaction did start right there, in a classroom. It came about as a result of dedicated school staff who were not satisfied with the teaching methods then available, which felt too rigid, too directive, and most of all did not acknowledge of the developmental reality of their learners. This new way of teaching challenged traditional views on education. Forty years on, it feels as if these views have only just slightly shifted. Talking about the crucial importance of 'well-being' and of 'learning to be social' is not enough – we must ensure our practice leads the way!

Because this book covers such a broad range of education settings, several terms are used throughout the book by different authors. You will find: 'children', 'students', 'pupils', and 'learners'; 'teachers', 'teaching assistants', 'staff', 'practitioners', and 'educators'. We hope that you will not be too side-tracked by these different descriptions and recognise that we have allowed authors to use the terms that come naturally to describe themselves, their colleagues, and the youngsters with whom they work. The book includes a glossary of terms to cover any technical language, and we have endeavoured to write in full any acronyms that are later included in the text. Perhaps the most important of these are the use of 'FoCs' for the 'Fundamentals of Communication' which are at the heart of Intensive Interaction. These are listed and explained in Chapter 3 for anyone new to this approach.

The book is designed both to be read cover to cover or for readers to be able to pick stand-alone chapters that are of direct relevance to their teaching situation (and hopefully then return to read the rest!). They are written in quite different styles, and we hope that adds to the book's pace and interest. Each chapter includes boxes with highlighted teaching points for easy reference.

The chapters focus upon different areas – working from Early Years Foundation Stages to Post-16 provision, including describing the use of Intensive Interaction throughout an all-age school, and management issues around its implementation. They explore the approach with autistic students, pupils with complex needs, severe learning difficulties, and profound and multiple learning disabilities. The key importance of Intensive Interaction for all students with special educational needs and disabilities (SEND) and the teaching and learning theories it encompasses are discussed. There are chapters which explore Intensive Interaction and play; considerations around touch; and using Intensive Interaction as a way of developing an individualised, process-central curriculum and integrating the approach into an established holistic curriculum. Excellent guidance and examples of good practice are included for writing Intensive Interaction into Education, Health and Care (EHC) Plans, Individual Learning Plans (ILPs) and recording. While the chapters are diverse, common themes repeat and run through the whole book like a golden thread.

We are hoping that this book will highlight that everyone involved in educating SEND students is key in changing the educational and social ecology around the child to thus prioritise and enable social communication learning. Within this group we warmly include numerous, dedicated and indefatigable home educators for whom Intensive Interaction forms the bedrock of their children's learning. The Intensive Interaction Institute offers both training and the support of like-minded professionals to help with this journey.

Let's be clear here . . . our mission with Intensive Interaction is not just the kind of progress a child can make in a term or in a year. In reality, this is a long-term investment for their whole future. Embracing the Intensive Interaction philosophy and ensuring it is at the heart of practice in schools will benefit the individual in the long-term and have profound and positive life-changing effects.

## Reference

Kellet, M. and Nind, M. (2003). *Implementing Intensive Interaction in Schools: Guidance for Practitioners, Managers and Co-ordinators*. Abingdon: David Fulton.

# 2. The story of Intensive Interaction

*Dave Hewett*

## In the beginning

Intensive Interaction started in classrooms. It started because we did not know what to teach. Actually, we realised later that we also did not know *how* to teach. We did not know what to teach to students who did not speak and were mostly seeming to be not motivated to relate much, or they simply did not seem to know how to be meaningfully social. Many clearly found the prospect of being social to be excruciatingly threatening. Quite a few of them were severely withdrawn into their own world of often rhythmical, persistent behaviour. They were all still operating at very early levels of development in every respect — cognitively, emotionally, psychologically, and of course, communicatively. Many, maybe most of them, had received diagnoses of autism. Many of them, many, were also — understandably, given their circumstances — capable of what we consider to be the most severely challenging behaviour. Some of them were people detained in secure accommodation under Section 3 of the Mental Health Act.

So, this was a very special, special school. It was nominally a usual local authority–administered school for children with severe learning difficulties but placed within the campus of a large, learning disability long-stay hospital in Hertfordshire, just outside London. These places mostly no longer exist.

There was a diminishing number of children left in the hospital then, 1981–1982, when I started there as Deputy Headteacher. I became the Headteacher in 1983. The school had therefore actually become an informal further education establishment, working with teenagers and young adults. During the 1980s, national policy gradually turned against admitting children to these institutions as far as possible, but the hospital and the education authority made an agreement to maintain our service. We had evolved into specialists in working with people who may display 'challenging behaviours', or at least, specialists in managing to survive working with them, on the whole.

Thus, the majority of our students were physically active adult people who could be difficult to be around, or actually, they found it difficult to be around us — and each other. When they had their oh so frequent difficult times, being fully grown people, naturally, life became interesting for all of us. In my early days, I remember our team had a reasonable presence at the local casualty department. We also had several students with complex needs in a classroom in a quiet building in another part of the hospital. However, they too, of course, shared many of the same educational needs as our more active and volatile people — still at early levels of development in every respect.

DOI: 10.4324/9781003170839-2

Our main building was the former hospital tuberculosis ward; it was dilapidated, draughty, and serviced with dank, uncomfortable bathrooms at each end of a long corridor, bathrooms which, of course, were in frequent use. The building leaked, the heating broke down frequently, and we were poorly financed to replace the regularly smashed furniture.

Thus, we were the end of the line. Most of our students had gravitated to the hospital due to their behaviour. They were then accommodated in a lino, formica, and gloss paint environment of the hospital ward dormitories and looked after by an insufficient number of people wearing uniforms. If they were fortunate, they could receive education in our school, within a building unfit for use. We, the staff, were thus working within this terrible physical environment, with some of the most difficult people there are to be around. I loved it. Most of the team loved it. You had to.

There were some lovely, thoughtful, and reflective people in the team – both teachers and teaching assistants. I would emphasise here that all through this story, I will be describing what I consider to be a profound and meaningful educational initiative that came about due to the innovative work of the team – and that includes the teaching assistants. We were blessed with some wonderful personalities as the team evolved throughout that decade. The teaching assistants were just as important, just as innovative, just as reflective within a team that gradually learnt the skills of reflection influencing development. The teaching assistants too wrote records, came up with ideas, and offered challenging questions.

In the early days of 1981–1982, most of the workings of the curriculum were centred on the then common traditions of behaviourist approaches. One of the best known of the behaviourist scientists was B.F. Skinner, who developed the principles of 'operant conditioning' in experiments on rats and pigeons, starting in the 1930s. It is the work of Skinner that has had perhaps the greatest influence in special needs work, in its use to modify unwanted behaviours, in its application to attempt to train a person to adopt the behaviours of new skills using a rewards system. The well-known symbols approach called PECs, for instance, if applied as recommended, employs operant conditioning principles. There are many objections to the application of 'Skinnerite' principles. Indeed, an aspect of the motivation on my part for our work on Intensive Interaction was a desire to move away from the perception of a person as a behaviour mechanism which can be 'tweaked' by an observing and intervening authority. I, we, gradually desired to present more natural, collaborative, and joyful teaching and learning to people who are at very early levels of development which results in the growth of abilities, concepts, and attitudes.

> Behavioural approaches owe their heritage to the work of early psychologists such as John B. Watson in the 1910s–1920s, who desired that this very new field of psychology be accepted by the scientific community. Since the physical sciences mostly express their findings, the new 'facts', numerically, with

> statistics, the thinking of some of the early psychologists went in this direction. If you think about it, the only aspect of human experience that can reliably be observed and counted is external behaviour. Thus, the behaviourist branch of the then developing field of psychology started to focus more or less exclusively on observable, countable behaviours and ways in which the environment around a person might be 'tweaked' to change or modify the count of those behaviours. Now, of course, many of us these days find it incredible that a field of psychology should focus only on visible behaviour and have little interest in things like thoughts, feelings, and attitudes, but that is what happened.

So, in the beginning, our curriculum was, well, dour, serious, uninspired. We attempted to be controlling. We used behaviour modification to try to change behaviours we did not want, rather than do clever things to help the person change by developing. There was an overall focus on the training of new 'skills' using operant conditioning principles. We desired that our students would sit on chairs at tables and do 'cognitive' activities – inset puzzles, posting toys, stacking things, matching, and sorting. All these activities can bring somewhat useful achievements, but we started to question whether these were the priorities for people who did not know how to relate meaningfully and might have problems with a member of staff sitting near them. Indeed, many of our students were not at a stage of development where they could be relied upon to sit still on a chair for long – they had not yet found the motivation nor the purpose of the function of sitting at a table.

# Developmental reality and teaching priorities

Many of us in the team started having difficult but honest discussions. It started in the staffroom over our Tupperware boxes of sandwiches. Why do we do this – or that? Why do we give them inset puzzles over and over again? Why do we desperately need them to sit down when they find it so difficult? Surely the priority for all of them is communication, human communication? We all received training in Makaton, but most of our students were nowhere near being able to notice, understand, or use signing. This was one of the breakthrough discussions I remember, the realisation, the deep, proper educational perception that in terms of communication, most of our students were nowhere near being able to employ, nor see the point of, symbolic representation. This realisation started us on the pathway that we follow to this day – human communication is so much more than words.

At this time came the second big, breakthrough realisation which is again familiarly followed in the Intensive Interaction community to this day. Namely, how old are they really? We started to discuss that one of the main reasons so much of what we offered failed, Makaton, for instance, was due to the reality of our students' levels of development. Most of what we were doing was pitched too far ahead of them developmentally. When we really, really got down to the nitty gritty of our students' abilities and understandings, we made the breakthrough into the positivity of another big realisation that was necessary for us to accept. Even though they were adults, even though many of our students were physically adept in so many ways, operationally, cognitively, psychologically, and emotionally most were still operating at a less than one-year level. Many at a very much less than one-year level. That is why they found speech or Makaton so difficult – they were nowhere near that level developmentally. They needed to receive educational, developmental experiences that come before most of what we were offering. At the same time, therefore, it became necessary for us to seriously question the current orthodoxy of the time of an outlook such as 'age-appropriateness'. In any way strictly treating our students primarily through a focus of their chronological ages could not work. This outlook was losing them, missing them. It more or less guaranteed that they would not, could not, prosper.

We accepted the proposition that our students were mainly still at the earliest levels of development. That this was their reality. Wishing it to be different or working as if it was different was just stupid. We needed to be with them where they were 'at'. See a further discussion of notions of 'age-appropriateness' in Chapter 11.

These discussions were not easy, but I recommend them most highly. Always question, always review. Always be prepared to change. We found a relaxed position from which to view the landscape of our work. It became okay to say out loud that we had a lot of it badly wrong. Everything was easier then. We were able to articulate that much of what we did were the wrong things. We were able to admit that most of us were not comfortable working with behaviour modification and the sensation of the extreme imbalance of power and authority that came with it. We recognised that a lot of the time our classrooms were tense, reactive places, rather than relaxed, warm, and nurturing environments.

Given the developmental levels of the students, we gradually decided during discussion and early try-outs that we needed to create classrooms that were relaxed, warm, and nurturing. One or two of our classroom assistants had experience in early years' work and that assisted with a vision. We started openly to discuss the prospect that we needed to be providing daily experiences that were not so controlling moment by moment but rather more open, relaxed, peaceful, and fun. We needed to teach our students to be able to do something they probably had never done – to play. But even more profoundly we started to focus on the central learning need of our students: communication. Not speech, not symbols, not signs, but communication – interaction, connection.

Speech, symbols, and signs are useful aspects of the detail of communication, but they are the gloss of communication, not a summary of it. Our discussions kept returning to our unhappy experiences with Makaton and that developmental realisation. Most of our students were not at the level of symbolic representation. They needed developmental experiences which come before that and lead to it. Some of this was more difficult for the qualified teachers in the team. We had to accept and embrace the reality I have described in the first paragraph; we did not previously know what to teach to our students, and we did not know much about how to teach them.

We deliberately started on a pathway. Our discussions evolved into a resolve to change and move forward. We started to attempt to create the relaxed nurturing classrooms we fantasised. We agreed to keep trying things out, and we also agreed to have regular report and review meetings. We took decisions to relax the physical environments. There was a gradual easing of an emphasis on chairs and tables. They were still in the rooms, but the rooms gradually also comprised sofas, easy chairs, crash mats, and bean bags. There were more boxes of toys visible, yes, even for adults. The school had a large and pleasant garden area, and this became gradually a curriculum area, rather than a relief from it. We took decisions to relax the social environment. It became possible to hear loud noises of people having fun emanating from the classrooms, rather than noises of people experiencing distress.

Gradually, early years'-style play sessions were becoming a norm in the classrooms with the students more free and autonomous to move around, and the staff encouraging and motivating participation rather than enforcing it. We noticed quite quickly that there was an appreciable drop in incidents of challenging behaviour – students less stressed and happier, staff less stressed and happier. Play became visible. Most of the individuals in our team were joyful, playful, funny personalities, and there was evident relief in being freed up to exploit these aspects of their personalities.

We also became more scholarly. We did access the main, authoritative books on special education, looking for further advice. We did start to consult education and psychological journals, questing to find others who might have addressed these issues and provided some answers. We did not find anything that we were looking for, but the habit begun there of scholarly enquiry, became part of the underpinning of our process and remains so to this day.

Gradually within what could feel like more or less controlled, somewhat more chaotic classroom life, we started to realise that perhaps, through relaxed play-type activities, we were attaining better levels of shared attention with the students, better connections. We were receiving more laughter, more smiles, more face-to-face contact. We liked what we were doing, and so did the students it seemed. We started to construct some kind of understanding of what we were doing. We met and reviewed regularly and kept notes. We were learning to be reflective. At an early stage we thought about adopting a name for what we were doing, and we arrived at 'ACE' – Appropriate Communication Environment.

## Finding and defining an approach

It was on a rainy evening either in December 1982 or January 1983, I can't be precise, that with two of the team I went to the local teachers' centre for a meeting. Teachers' centres mostly no longer exist. They were local teacher support establishments with libraries, resources, courses, meeting rooms, and advisers – for teachers. Somewhere along the line, the people who manage these things decided they were superfluous. Present at the meeting were a few special educators to meet with Geraint Ephraim, a senior psychologist at Leavesden Hospital, a similar institution to Harperbury Hospital where we worked, but about ten miles away. Ephraim was a friendly, jovial, deeply intellectual sort who had been looking at something interesting. He had been reading the newly available psychological research on how babies learn to be communicators during their first year.

Ephraim had made the association between what this research was now revealing about natural human communication learning and the possibilities for helping people who were in many respects at the same very early developmental levels communicatively. He was trying out his thoughts and showed a very grainy black-and-white video of a member of staff rocking in harmony with another person. But the key thing for me was Ephraim's advice about that research on babies: *don't bother inventing something new if the way we all learn to be communicators will work.*

We took the advice and started reading that enlightening research, with the result that what was in there began feeding into our development of teaching and learning technique. There will be more detail on this elsewhere in this volume and, of course, in our other books on Intensive Interaction. Basically though, the research gave us a whole new awareness and a whole new vocabulary, together with whole new thoughts about curriculum.

> Parent-infant interaction research blossomed in the USA during the 1970s with the advent of video technology. This enabled the researchers to micro-analyse the flow of behaviour within first-year parent-infant interactions, wherein babies learn the incredible volume and complexity of communication knowledge and ability – and then speech.
>
> Basically, babies learn to interact during interactions. They are not shown, they are not instructed, they do not undergo operant conditioning; they learn by doing in partnership with adults, in relaxed and enjoyable experiential situations.

We needed to be working on the fundamental things that the infant learns before speech and language and which build towards those developments: giving and sharing pleasurable attention, use and understanding of eye contact, facial expressions, body language, using and understanding vocalisations, etc. The teaching needed to be taking place in playful, relaxed interactions where the teacher gently worked from and responded to the student's flow of behaviour, gradually building a repertoire of meaningful communication attainments through pleasurable repetition of the activities. Those interaction activities fitted beautifully into the more relaxed free flow of our new classroom processes. Then, of course, we very quickly realised that this teaching and learning would be totally unlike anything described in the books on special school curriculum and would be more or less the opposite of behavioural approaches.

I guess it was the immersion in the interaction research that generated the adoption of 'Intensive Interaction' as a title around this time, but the details of the discussion are lost to me. However, the development of Intensive Interaction over the next five years or more was not a streamlined, easy process. We started attaining the results with our students that we were hoping for, but we had to become even more observant and reflective about our technique. The hardest things we needed to learn, but the absolute key things, were around holding back, not producing too much behaviour ourselves during the interaction activities, and truly learning to let the student lead the interaction with us generating content and flow by responding. This was so different, so revolutionary, but most of our team were flexible, questing personalities and they were up for it.

> As you might all be aware, the teaching and learning routines within Intensive Interaction are still radically different from traditional approaches in special education. The main learning resource is the member of staff – face, voice, body language, sense of presence – and the approach works by process rather than the setting of objectives. See Chapter 4 for further technical explanation.

Another key occurrence came about late the next year. Most of that research on infants was carried out using micro-analysis of video recordings of interactions. We would often wish for a video camera so that we could look back on and analyse technique, but back then they were very expensive, very large pieces of kit. However, the first camcorders became available in 1983, and we got one the following year. That was lift-off. Some of the happiest times of my professional life were at Harperbury, in the afternoons after school, many of us crowding together into a little room where we had equipment set up for watching our videos – rewinding, freeze-framing, discussing, arguing – reflecting on and developing teaching and learning.

Our students continued to prosper socially, acquiring more facility with the Fundamentals of Communication, becoming more engaged, less challenging. Gradually, we generated an education for ourselves about how this new thing worked. Finding out the techniques involved an honest process of recognising the bits that worked and discarding those that did not. The video analysis was key in this.

In 1985, I was sent to the Cambridge Institute of Education to study for a year for an Advanced Diploma in Special Education. The support of the staff at the Cambridge Institute is another key aspect of the story of the approach. David Hopkins, Martin Rouse, Mel Ainscow, Mary Hope, I hope you read this and feel a warm glow.

The course gave considerable scope to pursue one's interests. I haunted the library, and the main university library, studying and studying, particularly books and journal articles on parent-infant interaction and human communication in general. My final dissertation was based on an action-research project on Intensive Interaction that I ran back at my school. Also in 1985, our school team was completed by the arrival of

Melanie Nind. She was straight out of the local teacher's college but already knew us from carrying out project work in our school during her final year. She chose to work with us when other, more glamorous schools were vying to enlist her. She was known to be a brilliant student and had two published articles in academic journals whilst still at college. She wanted to join us because she had already evolved her own specialism in the development of new communication teaching for those at the earliest levels of development. Totally unsurprisingly to all who worked with her, she is these days a professor of education at Southampton University.

Nind's energy and intellectual drive, and my now deeper knowledge from my course intensified the Intensive Interaction development process. By 1987, we felt we had a refined and understood model of the approach with results for the students way beyond our expectations of a few years earlier. We knew also that we had an approach that would matter to so many schools and the people within them.

## The dissemination of Intensive Interaction

In the 1980s, more people in schools read educational journals. It was usual to see them in school staff rooms, usual for teachers to read them. We started writing about our work. What we wrote about had been a whole-team enterprise, but Nind and myself were the writers. Our work started to be published in those journals, it caused interest, we started to receive enquiries and visits – and not just from schools; from the earliest there was a great deal of interest from adult services. We received invites to give workshops at other schools and establishments. We started to be invited to speak at national conferences on special needs work. Being able to give presentations fulsomely illustrated with videos of our work was a big new thing. Everyone could see our approach for real, see how it worked, see the results. There is not a way to overstate the importance of video to the creation and dissemination of Intensive Interaction.

Some of those conferences were a big learning curve for Nind and myself. We didn't realise the extent to which we were 'babes in the woods'. Our attitude was *'hey everybody, we've got this really interesting new thing that really works, let us show you it'*. At quite a few conferences we received the clear attitude from some, *'who the hell do you think you are?'* We did not anticipate the extent to which we would make parts of the learning disability work establishment uncomfortable. By this we mean some of those people who had organised their careers around behavioural approaches, some of those people who had organised their work around concepts of 'age-appropriateness'. We would face very hostile questioning and attempts to ridicule. It felt like some other practitioners or authorities actually hated us and what we were doing. But we learnt how to debate and survive this. On the other hand, of course, despite the dramatic effect such hostility can have on one, mostly we were positively received, with many practitioners sharing our outlook of: *'gosh, yes of course, this is what we should be doing'*. Indeed, we were creating a stir, and by 1990 Intensive Interaction and the work of our school was widely acknowledged around the UK.

In 1988, primarily at Nind's urging, we commenced two research projects within our school. We both registered to carry out part-time PhD research projects with the Cambridge Institute of Education. Nind's project was designed to demonstrate efficacy – Intensive Interaction works. My project was centred around understanding and writing the methodology of the approach. Most of the staff were involved in the projects and wrote data or took part in video sessions. It was an exciting time, but very hard work as the projects were on top of our usual work. Nind would receive her doctorate in 1993, me in 1994. The project work contributed hugely, of course, to the writing and publication of our first book in 1994.

## After Harperbury School

For all sorts of reasons, including illness, I departed Harperbury School and my headship at the end of 1990. Melanie also left to follow her pathway in further and higher education to professorship. However, she and I remained in stewardship of Intensive Interaction. Nind and I would continue to write and publish together for the next 15 years. I started independent work as a consultant, with my main focus the dissemination of Intensive Interaction. Thus, I commenced a career of travelling around the UK, giving workshops in many, many schools and adult services establishments.

I have focused the main body of this chapter on the development of Intensive Interaction within Harperbury School between 1981 and 1990. I think it is a really good story about what a team of practitioners could achieve together, with thought, discussion, and enterprise. I think it contains all sorts of points – food for thought that are still relevant today.

### Some points, food for thought

Do you, the reader, think we already know everything we need to know about how to teach the pupils who are the focus of this book?

Who are the people who should be working on the development of teaching and learning technique?

Does your school team have a regular habit of evaluation and reflection on teaching and learning?

Where are the other innovations like Intensive Interaction? You know, teacher innovations in classrooms that have then become widely known?

However, the story of the development of Intensive Interaction needs to speed up somewhat here, so I will shamefully condense the account of what has happened since this earlier developmental stage. There are many significant figures in the progress of our Intensive Interaction mission who will not gain mention here, and to them I apologise.

By 1995–1996, the sustained effort of giving many workshops and continuing to present at conferences, together with the stir created by our first book on Intensive Interaction (Nind and Hewett, 1994) was bringing tangible dividends. Intensive Interaction was even more generally known in all services, and there was an appreciable community of practitioners remaining in contact and indeed starting their own projects and producing research and publications. Our first book was recognised in the Times Educational Supplement book awards, and our second (Hewett and Nind, 1998) gathered together the experiences of members of our burgeoning community, chronicling their own work on Intensive Interaction. Many articles and books have followed these initial volumes, charting developments and offering practical advice and insights to all who wish to further their knowledge of Intensive Interaction. Key texts which may be of interest to readers include Nind and Hewett (2001); Firth, Berry and Irvine (2010); Hewett (2012) and Hewett (2018).

By 2000, there was a self-sustaining, informal Intensive Interaction community of committed practitioners around the UK. Speech and Language Therapist Cath Irvine and I organised the first national Intensive Interaction conference in 2002, and this led to further, more formal developments. Graham Firth attended, and he quickly became a key figure, organising subsequent yearly conferences and driving forward the growth of our Intensive Interaction organisation. Firth quickly gained the post of Intensive Interaction Project Leader for the NHS Trust in Leeds, becoming one of those people who dedicate their working lives to the further dissemination and development of Intensive Interaction.

Sarah Forde must be mentioned, or rather, her central contribution absolutely highlighted. She started as my part-time secretary/assistant in 1994 but became as committed to the cause as any of the practitioners. Her administrative, organisational and finance skills were also fundamental to the establishment of the organisation and guiding its subsequent transition in 2011 into the Intensive Interaction Institute, a not-for-profit company.

We started the official Intensive Interaction website in 2003, and it is now the banner and first port of call for an increasingly worldwide organisation (intensiveinteraction.org). Do visit our website and see the range of resources and support available. The Intensive Interaction Institute is presently transitioning into becoming a Community Interest Company. Awareness of the approach is expanding and developing due to the collaborative work of a committed team of practitioners, administrators, and relatives of people whose lives have been changed by Intensive Interaction.

Our work goes on. We wish to take the approach to everyone around the world who needs it.

# References

Firth, G., Berry, R. and Irvine, C. (2010). *Understanding Intensive Interaction*. London: Jessica Kingsley.

Hewett, D. (ed.) (2012). *Intensive Interaction: Theoretical Perspectives*. London: Sage Publications.

Hewett, D. (ed.) (2018). *The Intensive Interaction Handbook*. 2nd ed. London: Sage Publications.

Hewett, D. and Nind, M. (eds.) (1998). *Interaction in Action: Reflections on the Use of Intensive Interaction*. London: David Fulton.

Nind, M. and Hewett, D. (1994). *Access to Communication: Developing the Basics of Communication with People with Severe Learning Difficulties Through Intensive Interaction*. London: David Fulton.

Nind, M. and Hewett, D. (2001). *A Practical Guide to Intensive Interaction*. Kidderminster: British Institute of Learning Disabilities.

# 3. What do students with autism and learning disabilities need to learn?

*Pam Smith*

As teachers educating students with special educational needs and disabilities (SEND), we work with a hugely diverse range of children and young people. Our relationships are built upon knowing them fully as individuals with unique personalities, preferences, strengths, interests, cultures, and life experiences. No single educational curriculum can possibly prepare students of such diversity for every opportunity and challenge they may meet in their lives. Similarly, in 30 years of working as a teacher of autistic children, pupils with severe learning difficulties (SLD), profound and multiple learning disabilities (PMLD), and complex needs I have never found two students who needed identical approaches to teaching and learning (not even twins!).

However, I have come to understand that every student's learning is built upon the bedrock of the Fundamentals of Communication (FoCs) (Nind and Hewett, 1994). These are the most important learning for all human beings and enhance every aspect of a person's life. This chapter will explore why the FoCs are essential learning for our students with SEND; the impact upon children and young people who find this learning difficult and how they can be supported by an Intensive Interaction approach.

## The importance of being socially connected

Human beings are social animals. We are connected through our families, friends, work colleagues, faith communities, interest groups, sports activities, pubs, clubs, bands, choirs – the list is endless. Being socially isolated is highly detrimental to mental health, and the enforced social isolation through COVID-19 lockdowns led to extreme distress (Mental Health Foundation, 2020; National Autistic Society, 2020). People were driven to extraordinary lengths to maintain social contact, from online meet-ups to heart-breaking 'window visits' with vulnerable and elderly relatives. Concern for our children's welfare went beyond their lost education to the negative social impact of missing school (Carpenter and Carpenter, 2020; Rae, 2020). We are driven to be social, and if we are deprived of human contact we fail to thrive (Hewett, 2012a).

## The social journey begins – chemistry, neuroscience, and social junkies

Our drive to be social begins before birth (see Chapter 11) and develops thereafter through the numerous incidental, loving interactions that naturally occur between babies and their caregivers. Countless unplanned, spontaneous activities form loving, trusting bonds and develop the enjoyment of social connectivity. In her 'Social Thinking' publications and training Garcia Winner (2021) reiterates that no one teaches us how to be social – most typically developing children develop these skills automatically. Rubin (2017) explains this by describing neurotypical babies as 'social junkies', whose brains' social centres flood with dopamine as they look towards and engage with their caregivers (Chevallier et al., 2012). This dopamine rush drives them to seek out more social interactions, and their communication skills develop and increase exponentially with repeated daily practice.

In Chapter 2, Hewett describes how studies of the natural model of mother and baby interactions influenced the development of Intensive Interaction as a process. Analysis of these dyadic exchanges documented how effortlessly typically developing infants learned about communication and social communication, enhanced by the caregivers' attentive, tuned-in responses (Zeedyk, 2012). The mutual pleasure gained within these exchanges was all-encompassing, forming a timeless communication 'bubble' outside of which nothing else seemed to exist.

Arredondo (2009, 2011) has analysed the neurological impact of infant–caregiver interactions. He describes how as mother and baby gaze at one another, 'their eyes, ... brains, hearts and minds are connected' in a shared emotional state of 'attunement'. During this 'deep, genuine and significant connection with another human', the infant's brain forms 1000 neural connections per second. Arredondo describes these pleasurable communication moments, feeling loved and cherished as 'critical learning for human development' (ibid., 2011). This is the essence of the FoCs.

## Barriers to learning to communicate using the 'natural model' for children with SEND

The social communication learning acquired so easily by neurotypical infants via the 'natural model' (Chapter 2) can be much more difficult for our students with SEND, who frequently have multiple barriers to overcome. Research has shown that, through no fault of their parents, interactions may be disrupted by several issues. Extreme circumstances, such as birth trauma, may mean the infant is too poorly to be held or may only be able to leave an incubator for restricted amounts of time. Premature babies' sensory systems operate on high alert, making it difficult to interact without causing sensory overload (Crayne, 2017).

A baby with learning difficulties may be less responsive and have more difficulties in synchronising exchanges with their mother (Rogers, 1988). Other infants may be neurologically differently wired and may not register the same flood of dopamine described earlier, leading to a weaker drive for seeking social reinforcement (Chevallier et al., 2012).

These early life experiences can create major barriers for SEND students around learning the FoCs. Imray and Colley (2017) identified that the additional challenges experienced by children with SLD and PMLD have a major impact upon communication, concentration, shared attention, sequential memory, processing speeds, and problem solving. Many of these problems are shared by children with other learning disabilities and autism, especially those with impaired executive function and sensory dysregulation (Curran, 2008). However, neural plasticity allows for new pathways to be established through repeated practice and overlearning (Zeedyk, 2012), and the impact of these barriers can be reduced through offering multiple opportunities to develop the FoCs through an Intensive Interaction approach.

Considering the importance of the FoCs and their impact on learning, it is worth thinking about what we currently teach our students and where our priority as teachers should lie.

## What do we teach students with SEND and why – broad and balanced or focused learning?

To get the whole picture of what we teach our SEND students and why, we need to look back to the Warnock Report (1978). This truly ground-breaking document introduced the term 'children with learning disabilities' for the first time, cited parents as partners in their child's education, and championed inclusion as a means of overcoming prejudice against disability and difference. It also offered new educational opportunities to children formerly labelled 'ineducable' and spoke of education led by children's needs. The recommendations led to the 1981 Education Act with provision for children with special education needs and, 40 years later, had a major influence on the SEND Code of Practice (Department for Education – DfE and Department of Health – DoH, 2015; Webster, 2018).

The guidelines specifying what we must teach our SEND students can appear a little overwhelming. The Code of Practice states that SEND children are entitled to a broad and balanced curriculum. The Rochford Review (Standards and Testing Agency – STA, 2016) and Engagement Model (STA, 2020) advocate individualised, personalised learning pathways. Safeguarding guidelines (DfE, 2020) emphasise teachers' responsibility for promoting children's mental and emotional well-being. In addition, many SEND students have a statutory Education, Health and Care (EHC) Plan, identifying their cognition and learning; communication and interaction; social, emotional, and mental health difficulties; and sensory and/or physical needs.

Without wishing to appear flippant, this shopping list of requirements suggests that teachers must provide each of their diverse SEND students with a curriculum which is simultaneously broad and balanced but individualised and personalised; safeguards their mental and physical health and well-being and meets their therapy needs whilst ensuring progress is achieved, tracked, evidenced, and reported on their EHC Plan targets (DfE, 2020; STA, 2020). No wonder teachers are exhausted! On a serious note, this daunting task is indeed possible if we put our students and their individual needs firmly at the centre. However, it demands great skill and reflective practice to ensure we maintain this child-centred focus and avoid simply ticking boxes and rushing on to the next activity to get through a full and busily timetabled day.

There are many statutory and external demands (including Ofsted) upon what and how we should teach our SEND students (see Chapter 12). But we, as their teachers, also need to have a clear vision of what and how they need to learn. The principles of individualised and personalised learning give us permission to be truly child-centred. However, we need to consider carefully what the words 'broad and balanced curriculum' really mean for our students.

Many of our students are at a developmentally early stage of learning. They may be enduring severe behavioural challenges due to sensory overload, anxiety, trauma, or impaired well-being. Rather than breadth and balance, we must ask ourselves if these students might benefit from a narrower focus of learning (discussed further in Chapter 4). This is not intended to impoverish their lives or discriminate against their educational rights but to focus upon their primary need for deep, developmentally pertinent learning.

## Putting the Fundamentals of Communication at the heart of all learning

Communication informs, underpins, and gives access to all other aspects of learning and the curriculum. If the FoCs are not learnt, all other learning is disrupted, and the child is disadvantaged emotionally, socially, and cognitively (Nind, 2012). We therefore need to put the FoCs at the heart of *all* learning for our SEND students.

There seems to be some confusion about which students need Intensive Interaction in their curriculum and on their EHC Plans. My response is: all our SEND students 'need' Intensive Interaction, regardless of age and cognitive ability. In the case of autistic students, I would also add regardless of their verbal abilities.

I am sure we all know autistic students who read fluently but have difficulty explaining the story or who watch videos showing social scenarios and cannot unpick the meaning or who speak fluently and

# What do students need to learn?

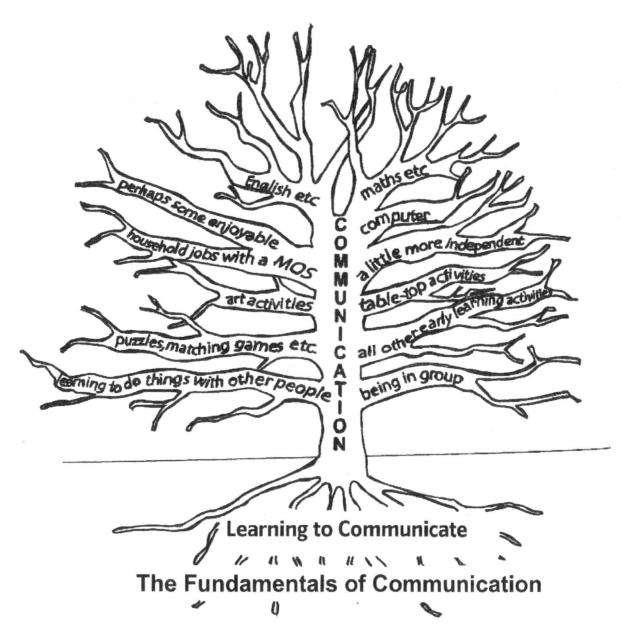

'Learning the ability to communicate and relate is the root formation, with communication then being the trunk that supports all other performances and attainments' (Hewett, 2018, p. 82).

**Figure 3.1** The Communication Tree (Hewett, 2018, p. 84).

intelligently about their specialist interests but struggle with small talk and find themselves socially isolated. Social attention, understanding social context and social communication remain a lifelong core difficulty of autism. Learning and practicing the FoCs in different contexts offers constant, much-needed support throughout their lives – I say this with love and respect as the mother of an autistic adult, who, despite studying for a Master's degree in opera, still finds the social side of life baffling, difficult, and totally exhausting!

Intensive Interaction is unique among other school-based approaches to developing communication. It underpins every other approach by working at the earliest stage of communication development (see Chapter 7) – by joining our SEND students in their world we help them begin to understand communication as a two-way process. Also, Intensive Interaction focuses on phatic rather than functional communication. Phatic and functional communication have distinctly different objectives. Put simply, functional communication always has a purpose and outcome: e.g. 'I want biscuit'. Phatic communication, also known as chit chat or small talk – e.g. 'Did you see that beautiful sunset yesterday?' – has no tangible outcome other than social engagement. Phatic communication builds relationships and develops awareness of how to fit in with the social world. In short, it is the social glue that holds society together. Through Intensive Interaction we develop phatic communication, build trust and the enjoyment of being with another person, and develop awareness of communicating just for fun (Hewett, 2012a).

The Engagement Model encourages us to get to know our SEND students so we can meet their academic needs. While we welcome this perspective, I think everyone will agree that human relationships are so much more than facilitating accurate progress assessment and target setting! We want our students to feel comfortable with us in school, but we also need to help them develop their own friendships, relationships, and life-long skills. The Code of Practice states that children with SEND should: *'achieve successful long-term outcomes in adult life . . . including having friends and supportive relationships'* (p. 28). We therefore need to offer learning which will support them to interact positively with others and to make and maintain friendships. From the child's point of view, forming relationships, learning to be with another person, sharing space and enjoying their company is the most important learning they will ever do (Nind, 2012; Firth, 2012) and can truly be described as a universal human right (Hewett et al., 2019).

## Why are the Fundamentals of Communication so important?

The FoCs can appear to be a list of discrete skills but nothing could be further from the truth. We need to explore why they are so important to our SEND students, how they underpin other learning, and what this looks like from a practical perspective. The FoCs are not listed hierarchically or as stand-alone elements. They represent the hugely complex and interrelated aspects of communication learning that can be seen. But, like an iceberg, underneath there is much more going on – huge amounts of unseen rich learning forming those 1000 neural connections per second.

We should also acknowledge that some of our students are so complex that getting to know them is not always straightforward. So, let's break down how we can start building these vital relationships and trust through rehearsing and learning the all-important FoCs. Throughout this book, you will find case studies which give examples of these in practice.

# Fundamentals of Communication 1 – communication / social communication

- Enjoying being with another person.
- Developing the ability to attend to that person.
- Developing concentration and attention span.
- Learning to do sequences of activity with the other person.
- Sharing personal space.
- Using and understanding eye contacts (face and mind reading).
- Using and understanding facial expressions.
- Using and understanding physical contacts (touch policy).
- Using and understanding non-verbal communication.
- Using vocalisations with meaning (for some individuals possibly speech development).

# Breaking down the Fundamentals of Communication 1 – communication and social interaction

### Enjoying being with another person

Building a rapport with your student, helping them to feel comfortable with you in their space and enjoy spending time together is the earliest but most crucial element of your Intensive Interaction journey together. So, before you start this journey, take some time to get to know them. This may sound a strange thing to say as you may already have worked with them for a while, but take this time to really observe them closely and consider how you might join their world and spend time tuning into them as an individual. Video these observations so you can watch them more than once and use them as baseline recording (see Appendices 1 and 2). For more detailed observation advice see Chapters 6, 10 and 14.

### Sharing personal space

When you begin Intensive Interaction, your student may simply be starting to learn about tolerating and becoming comfortable with another person in their space. Try to be open minded and have no expectations or pre-conceptions of what the session should feel like or be. It will be as it is on the day! The session length will depend on the individual student's response. It could last a few seconds or several minutes – both are fine. Important skills are being learnt just by enjoying time and 'hanging out' together, laying the foundations for emotional regulation.

> Sharing space can be really challenging for some of our students, especially if they are unsure of what is going to happen or is expected of them. So, it is worth thinking through some strategies to try if a student becomes anxious or distressed:
>
> - Check your distance – move farther away and see if that helps.
> - Check your position – try getting lower, adjust so you are next to the student or at a 45-degree angle, not facing them.
> - Wait and pause . . . and wait and pause . . . and wait and pause – give processing time.
> - Drop your gaze – some students find eye-contact uncomfortable or even intimidating.
> - Be available – open body language, accepting and warm facial expression.
> - Make sure your body language is really relaxed – practice calm breathing.
> - Keep your responses really small, subtle, and slow – maybe even just lifting an eyebrow or sighing in response to theirs.
> - Convey that you have all the time in the world – be unrushed and fully focused.
> - Stay alert in case you need a quick exit!

Some students have learnt to be prompt-dependent and may initially become highly anxious or confused about taking the lead if you do nothing. However, knowing that they are in charge and leading the session is essential learning. Support them through this with relaxed body language, confidence, and quiet patience until they feel comfortable. This is when the learning truly begins. Please don't give up or take it personally. If they become unsettled, thank them for their time and finish the session. Try again another day.

### Developing the ability to attend to another person

Attention is crucial to all learning, and students need to learn where to direct their focus. Some autistic students may be able to attend happily to a toy or special interest for several minutes; but we are interested in social attention – their ability to attend to a person rather than 'stuff'. Their attention may be fleeting at first, but keep persevering. As sessions become more established, the student will start to pay attention to you, and over time you will help them learn that you are even more interesting than their special object!

### Developing concentration and attention span

Through frequent practice and rehearsal, the student's attention on you and your shared activities will start to become more sustained. You may also see signs of increased concentration – both are essential prerequisites to all other learning. The student continues to lead so that the content, tempo, and dynamics of the interactions are always 'just right' for them. Allow plenty of time for pausing and waiting for them to be ready to reinitiate or re-engage. Their ability to attend and concentrate will enable interactions to be sustained for longer and for deeper learning of the FoCs to start to develop.

## Learning to do sequences of activity with the other person

Students start to learn the power of leading communication when sequences become established and begin to develop a feeling of give and take. There may be more exchanges of purposeful actions (tapping on a tray, rocking the body) as they recognise you are joining in. They may start playing the 'yes, but can you do this...?' game, varying their activities by tapping loudly or quietly, making different vocalisations or mouth shapes, crossing and uncrossing their legs – just to test you out!

As the interaction develops, shared actions, vocalisations, or activities may start to increase in intensity, frequency, or duration, leading to greater shared focus and attention. An easy 'tennis rally' style starts to develop – these back-and-forth exchanges are essential, preceding turn-taking and, ultimately, conversation. Sequences of student-led exchanges may start to build. The content of these sequences of activity will differ enormously depending upon the individual. They may be repetitive for extended periods of time or may develop new elements. Stay tuned in, watch out for these, and be ready to run with them and respond. Just a note that you may need to do your homework when using autistic students' special interests for these exchanges. Topics I have had to learn include Formula 1, obscure American folk bands, Greek and Roman mythology, Pokémon (and all their evolutions), Marvel superheroes, manga, and anime.

## Learning complex skills in a demand-free situation

Intensive Interaction offers opportunities for learning about complex social communication skills, such as non-verbal communication, physical contacts, and facial expressions in a safe and enjoyable situation. Eye contact, which can be so challenging for some of our students, may develop naturally in this relaxed, trusting situation. Learning is pleasurable, low demand, and error-free, and students' stress levels reduce accordingly. The key importance of touch, physical contact, and non-verbal communication within Intensive Interaction cannot be overemphasised, and these are discussed in detail in Chapter 11.

## Using vocalisations with meaning

Vocalisations may start as breaths or tiny sounds which the practitioner can respond to and reflect back to the student. Given time and space to realise that the sounds are theirs, a student may start to react and respond consistently. After repeated practice they may begin to process that this exchange is intentional and different sounds, tones, and vocalisations may emerge. Favourite songs, words, or phrases may become key parts of turn-taking sequences or expressing emotions.

The principles of pausing and waiting remain essential, and we should always give our students time to initiate or respond. Although waiting can make us feel uncomfortable, and it can be tempting to jump in and fill a silence, always bear in mind that the less we do, the more room there is for the student to respond (Hewett, 2018).

> # Fundamentals of Communication 2 – emotional learning
>
> - Knowing that others *care*, learning to care.
> - Enjoying being with another person – connecting, bonding.
> - Attachment, attunement.
> - Self-security, to feel safe, secure, calm.
> - Self-esteem, sense of self.
> - To identify own feelings and see the same in others.
> - Gradually to understand feelings.
> - Trust stuff etc.
> - Empathy, knowing/caring about how somebody else feels.
> - Right-hemisphere brain development (early emotional learning prepares areas of the brain for later, higher functions).

# Breaking down the Fundamentals of Communication 2 – emotional learning

Emotional learning is key for all our SEND children. It is impossible to unpick these strands or to work out if they precede, follow, or develop simultaneously alongside communication/social communication learning as they are so closely intertwined (Hewett, 2012b).

In Chapter 7, the authors describe Maslow's theory of how basic human requirements that drive our motivation must be met before individuals can be ready to learn (Maslow, 1943). Once a child's physical needs are met, Intensive Interaction supports them with learning to feel safe and loved and to develop a sense of belonging. Learning the FoCs can develop esteem and self-actualisation (this means someone is able to develop themselves and their potential abilities to the fullest extent) through self-expression. This is especially valuable for our premature or low–birth weight SEND students who are particularly vulnerable to reactive attachment disorder and impaired social interactions (Upadhyaya et al., 2020; Geddes, 2020).

High anxiety, sensory overload, and trauma have severe negative effects on learning for SEND students who are stuck in 'fight, flight, or freeze' mode (Porges, 2011; McDonnell, 2020). It is essential for these students to be supported to learn ways of regulating their emotions, as if they are emotionally dysregulated, the cognitive areas of their brain will not be accessible for learning (Curran, 2008; Siegel,

2012). Intensive Interaction helps develop safety cues and feelings of calmness and security, fostering a greater readiness to learn.

Beyond school, emotional regulation is an essential life skill which opens opportunities for living independently, forming relationships, studying, and managing daily demands. Through Intensive Interaction we can help our students to build awareness of their feelings and emotions and to develop emotional co-regulation through experiencing excitement, calming down, and different emotional gradations. Learning and practicing the FoCs will support them long-term towards self-regulation. For our students with learning disabilities and autism this must surely be the most important learning of all.

## Top tips for successful Intensive Interaction

*Things that have proved valuable in my classroom practice*:

- A classroom with an embedded Intensive Interaction ethos embraces the principles throughout the day.
- When planning individual/class timetables, ringfence time so staff and resources can be allocated to 1:1 sessions; but never restrict Intensive Interaction to a 'communication' timetable slot – supplement planned sessions with naturally occurring incidental interactions.
- If a student doesn't appear interested or keeps leaving, go through your checklist:
  - Are you fully present and focused?
  - Can you do less, slow down?
  - Pause and wait – give processing time (10, 15, even 25 minutes is not unusual).
  - Check your posture, positioning, proximity, and body language.
  - Ensure students feel safe, connected, valued, and accepted.
  - If a student is agitated/distressed, try a larger comfort zone (Outside? Bigger space?).
  - Always keep yourself safe.
  - Accept things as they are and try again another day.
  - Don't take it personally – the student has social communication difficulties; it is hard for them!
  - Sessions may be joyful and exuberant, but reflective and quiet is good too. Be with them in their emotions.

Involve parents, family members and carers in Intensive Interaction with the student. The more the merrier!

# Final thoughts on moving on, repetition, and learning for life

I am often asked: 'How do I move them on?' My answer is usually: 'You don't – you support them to move themselves on!' As teachers we must learn to be patient, tuned in, receptive, and to trust in the process. It can sometimes be helpful to reflect on 'good practice' in other social situations. If things start becoming repetitive (which they will) and there is an urge to drive things forward by trying something new, think of going for a drink or a coffee with a friend who is going through a bad break up and only wants to talk about their ex. If it would be rude to say to them 'OK well, you've already told me that, so let's move on' or 'Not that again' or 'Can you just hurry up please, I want to get my lunch', then it is probably inappropriate to give those messages to the child during an Intensive Interaction session! Likewise, when finishing a session, be mindful of endings. We all prepare our friends when we need to leave a gathering and say goodbye. When finishing your time together, remember to thank them for being with you and say goodbye till next time.

Valuing the students in every aspect of our Intensive Interaction work creates a stronger bond between us. Through being respectful, nurturing, and always present with them in the moment, we convey that they are important to us and are a great person to spend time with. This is a powerful lesson for life.

# References

Arredondo, D. (2009). *Attunement and Why It Matters*. [video]. Available at: www.youtube.com/watch?v=URpuKgKt9kg [Accessed 27 November 2020].

Arredondo, D. (2011). *Attachment or Attunement?* [video]. Available at: www.youtube.com/watch?v=IGeS7o4FmRI [Accessed 27 November 2020].

Carpenter, B. and Carpenter, M. (2020). *A Recovery Curriculum: Loss and Life for Our Children and Schools Post Pandemic*. Available at: www.barrycarpentereducation.com [Accessed 18 February 2021].

Chevallier, C., Kohls, G., Troiani, V., Brodkin, E. S. and Schultz, R. T. (2012). The social motivation theory of autism. *Trends in Cognitive Science*, 16(4), pp. 231–239.

Crayne, R. M. (2017). *Interacting with Your Premature Infant: Developmental Care in the NICU*. Available at: https://wehavekids.com/parenting/Interacting-With-Premature-Infant-Developmental-Care-NICU [Accessed 27 November 2020].

Curran, A. (2008). *Little Book of Big Stuff About the Brain*. London: Crown House Publishing; Independent Thinking Series.

Department for Education (DfE), (2020). *Keeping Children Safe in Education*. Available at: www.gov.uk/government/publications/keeping-children-safe-in-education-2 [Accessed 27 November 2020].

Department for Education (DfE) and Department of Health (DoH), (2015). *Special Educational Needs and Disability Code of Practice: 0 to 25 Years*. Available at: www.gov.uk/government/publications/send-code-of-practice-0-to-25 [Accessed 6 November 2020].

Firth, G. (2012). 'Intensive Interaction for inclusion and development'. In: D. Hewett, ed., *Intensive Interaction Theoretical Perspectives*, 1st ed. London: Sage Publications, pp. 104–120.

Garcia Winner, M. (2021). *Social Thinking*. Available at: www.socialthinking.com [Accessed 16 February 2021].

Geddes, H. (2020). *Attachment in the Classroom*. 6th ed. London: Worth.

Hewett, D. (2012a). 'Blind frogs: The nature of human communication and Intensive Interaction'. In: D. Hewett, ed., *Intensive Interaction Theoretical Perspectives*, 1st ed. London: Sage Publications, pp. 4–21.

Hewett, D. (2012b). 'What is Intensive Interaction? Curriculum, process and approach'. In: D. Hewett, ed., *Intensive Interaction Theoretical Perspectives*, 1st ed. London: Sage Publications, pp. 137–154.

Hewett, D. (2018). 'Further and continuing progress'. In: D. Hewett, ed., *The Intensive Interaction Handbook*, 2nd ed. London: Sage Publications, pp. 65–84.

Hewett, D., Calveley, J., McKim, J. and Mourière, A. (2019). Communication, human rights and Intensive Interaction. *PMLD Link*, 31(1), Issue 92, pp. 8–10.

Imray, P. and Colley, A. (2017). *Inclusion Is Dead*. London: Routledge.

Maslow, A. H. (1943). A theory of human motivation. *Psychological Review*, 50(4), pp. 370–396.

McDonnell, A. (2020). *Distressed behaviour: Understanding your child*.

Mental Health Foundation, (2020). *Loneliness During Coronavirus*. Available at: www.mentalhealth.org.uk/coronavirus/loneliness-during-coronavirus [Accessed 1 January 2021].

National Autistic Society, (2020). *Left Stranded: The Impact of Coronavirus on Autistic People and Their Families in the UK*. London: NAS. Available at: www.autism.org.uk/what-we-do/news/coronavirus-report [Accessed 1 January 2021].

Nind, M. (2012). 'Intensive Interaction, emotional development and emotional well-being'. In: D. Hewett, ed., *Intensive Interaction Theoretical Perspectives*, 1st ed. London: Sage Publications, pp. 22–38.

Nind, M. and Hewett, D. (1994). *Access to Communication: Developing the Basics of Communication with People with Severe Learning Difficulties Through Intensive Interaction*. London: David Fulton.

Porges, S. W. (2011). *The Polyvagal Theory: Neurophysiological Foundations of Emotions, Attachment, Communication, Self-Regulation*. New York: W. W. Norton and Company.

Rae, T. (2020). *A Toolbox of Wellbeing: Helpful Strategies and Activities for Children, Teens, Their Carers and Teachers*. Banbury: Hinton House.

Rogers, S. (1988). Characteristics of social interactions between mothers and their disabled infants: A review. *Child: Care, Health and Development*, 14, pp. 301–317.

Rubin, E. (2017). *The neuroscience of social competence in children with autism and social emotional learning difficulties.*

Siegel, D. (2012). *"Flipping Your Lid:" A Scientific Explanation.* [video]. Available at: www.youtube.com/watch?v=G0T_2NNoC68 [Accessed 1 January 2021].

Standards and Testing Agency (STA), (2016). *The Rochford Review: Final Report Review of Assessment for Pupils Working Below the Standard of National Curriculum Tests.* Available at: https://assets.publishing.service.gov.uk/government/uploads/system/uploads/attachment_data/file/561411/Rochford_Review_Report_v5_PFDA.pdf [Accessed 27 November 2020].

Standards and Testing Agency (STA), (2020). *The Engagement Model Guidance for Maintained Schools, Academies (Including Free Schools) and Local Authorities.* Available at: www.evidenceforlearning.net/wp-content/uploads/2020/06/The_engagement_model_guidance_for_maintained_schools_academies_free_schools_and_local_authorities.pdf [Accessed 27 November 2020].

Upadhyaya, S., Chudal, R., Luntamo, T., Hinkka-Yli-Salomäki, S., Sucksdorff, M., Lehtonen, L. and Sourander, A. (2020). Perinatal risk factors and reactive attachment disorder: A nationwide population-based study. *Acta paediatrica* (Oslo, Norway: 1992), 109(8), pp. 1603–1611. Available at: https://doi.org/10.1111/apa.15156 [Accessed 25 February 2021]

Warnock, M. (1978). *Special Educational Needs: Report of the Committee of Enquiry into the Education of Handicapped Children and Young People.* London: Her Majesty's Stationery Office. Available at: www.educationengland.org.uk/documents/warnock/warnock1978.html [Accessed 6 November 2020].

Webster, R. (2018). *Why the Warnock Report Still Matters Today.* UK: TES. Available at: www.tes.com/news/why-warnock-report-still-matters-today [Accessed 27 November 2020].

Zeedyk, S. (2012). 'Wired for communication: How the neuroscience of infancy helps in understanding the effectiveness of Intensive Interaction'. In: D. Hewett, ed., *Intensive Interaction Theoretical Perspectives*, 1st ed. London: Sage Publications, pp. 55–71.

# 4. Intensive Interaction as a teaching and learning approach

*Amandine Mourière*

I started working as a teaching assistant in 2010. I did not know anything about special education at that time, but I quickly grew to love working with children in this setting. These children did not fit into the traditional school model but nonetheless were able to learn and flourish. And here is what I came to realise: their access to education relied on our appreciation of their uniqueness and consequently our teaching practices to enable their access to education. Over the last 12 years, I slowly learnt about the complex issues teaching staff are faced with when it comes to teaching and learning. This chapter offers a theoretical perspective which aims at giving you some of the tools and foundations to challenge the status quo and, I hope, the means to implement changes on a practical level.

## How Intensive Interaction challenges traditional views on teaching

Since different aspects of learning call for different methods of teaching, this section will look specifically at what teaching means in respect to learning the social-communication skills and abilities which support and enable human beings to interact and create meaningful connections. In Chapter 3, Pam Smith defined the learning priorities for children with autism and those with learning disabilities, highlighting the crucial importance of the Fundamentals of Communication (FoCs) as a foundation for subsequent learning.

The first steps of learning within typical development are the FoCs, and by the time a child is 3 years of age, they have acquired a solid foundation of communication abilities and cognitive developments on which to build other skills and abilities. Though we don't really think about it this way, babies are taught from day one within their interactions with tuned-in caregivers who synchronise their responses to support and scaffold their communicative attainments (Devouche and Gratier, 2019). The environment and style for 'successful teaching' at this level of development has been informed by the research on parent-infant interaction in the 1970s. It outlines how human beings learn to communicate and how foundational this learning is for them to fulfil their potential as they grow older. The findings from this bulk of research changed the way human development was understood. It allowed researchers to understand the optimal conditions under which babies thrive. Also, to appreciate that for the type of learning that babies do, the

DOI: 10.4324/9781003170839-4

teaching approach differs greatly from traditional methods in education. Intensive Interaction strongly suggests that all educationists should have the insight to go beyond our traditions and learn from what this research has revealed.

## Curriculum

Defining the areas of learning pupils need to access and how this learning is going to be facilitated is therefore of utmost priority. These two fundamental aspects of education are set out in the school curriculum. Before going any further, the term 'curriculum' needs some clarification, especially in the context of education and special education. The national curriculum (Department for Education, DfE, 2014) sets out specific programs and attainment targets for all subjects, whilst Special Educational Needs and Disabilities (SEND) schools are entrusted with the responsibility to design their own curriculum to reflect the reality of their learners' educational needs. This can be a daunting task for schools, with grey areas and uncertainties about what to do for the best. There is a danger that if the curriculum is not well-defined, the learning outcomes and teaching practices that will derive from it may not be in line with the learners' developmental needs.

> It is for these reasons that it is paramount for schools and teachers to define what is meant by 'curriculum', bearing in mind that the SEND Code of Practice (DfE, 2015) stipulates that:
>
> *'children with special educational needs should be offered full access to a broad, balanced and relevant education, including an appropriate curriculum for the foundation stage and the National Curriculum'.*
>
> *(p. 13)*

Given the need advocated in this book to prioritise social-communication learning, the curriculum design needs to be given careful thought. Depending on the children's cognitive abilities, the task at hand can become a balancing act between a learner-centred curriculum to give access to foundation stage learning and a subject-centred curriculum that focuses on academic learning.

For typically developing children, social-communication learning occurs within what can be defined as the 'natural curriculum', all the things they learn from being part of a family (Tharp and Gallimore, 1988). This is then developed by the 'hidden curriculum', which refers to the socialisation process of schooling (Kentli, 2009). By interacting with members of staff and other pupils, children get access to a gradually wider social ecology (Bronfenbrenner, 1979). This is an experiential process by which they learn about their culture, values within this culture, attitudes, and principles. The hidden curriculum is a critical aspect of a child's education. The learning outcomes are not intended by the teacher nor recognised by the curriculum. However, throughout their schooling children will be immersed in social activities promoting interpersonal interactions and facilitating intersubjectivity, key aspects of human connection enabling them to learn how to be in the world.

Increasingly, though, it is acknowledged that a school curriculum that focuses primarily on acquiring knowledge is not sufficient. Recognising emotional intelligence (Goleman, 1995) within the curriculum is essential since teachers are influential and powerful models. Therefore, their own embodiment of self-awareness, empathy, and self-management is required at a conscious level in order to facilitate these outcomes in the learners.

For the pupils we have in mind, social-communication is at the core of their difficulties. This means that the learning that occurs within the hidden curriculum is clearly not going to be enough. The learning of the FoCs cannot be overlooked, in the hope that perhaps these learning outcomes may be acquired incidentally as a result of good teaching practice. These learners may still be able to access other learnings, but unless concerted efforts are made to address their core impairments, they will never fully learn how to be in the world and will therefore be further impaired. Failing to access this foundational learning will have detrimental and damaging consequences on their mental health, their well-being, and their being in the social world (Hewett, 2012a). It is crucial for teaching staff to be supported and made aware of their responsibilities in ensuring that this learning is being recognised and prioritised (Kelly, 2009; Standards and Testing Agency, 2020).

> In a nutshell, the curriculum should encompass 'the totality of the experiences the pupil has as a result of the provision made' (Kelly, 2009, p. 8), acknowledging that the hidden curriculum needs to be visible for children with social-communication difficulties. Thus, the next dimension of a curriculum is to define how the learning outcomes described in the curriculum will subsequently be facilitated. Which brings us to an important aspect of teaching practice: pedagogy – the teaching approach a teacher adopts to reflect the reality of the learning outcomes.

## Pedagogy

When it comes to teaching pupils with social-communication difficulties, there seem to be conflicting messages and misconceptions about teaching practices being driven by the learner's age instead of learners' developmental reality.

Learners with social-communication difficulties are still likely to be at early levels of development as communicators, therefore they need a teaching approach which reflects this developmental reality. The model for teaching emotional and social-communication skills and abilities is well understood for typically developing children, with the bulk of the learning/development in these areas occurring in the first five years of a child's life. This critical developmental period is acknowledged in early-years education. It is at the very core of its philosophical underpinning: child-centred, rooted in play or self-initiated activities, rather than passively receiving direct instruction from adults. The pedagogy is play-based; creating a responsive environment for children to construct their learning, supported by nurturing adults. The Early Years Foundation Stages (EYFS) fully appreciate and recognise the developmental reality of early-years learners. The EYFS framework is designed for typically developing children between the ages of 0 and 5 and recognises the crucial importance of developing emotional and psychological resilience as a foundation for subsequent learnings. This framework was published by the Department for Children, Schools and Families in 2008 aiming at delivering consistent and high-quality environments for all children in pre-school settings. In 2017, it was made mandatory for all early-years providers in England (DfE, 2017).

The framework recognises three prime areas, stating that they 'are particularly crucial for igniting children's curiosity and enthusiasm for learning, and for building their capacity to learn, form relationships and thrive' (ibid., p. 7):

- Communication and language.
- Physical development.
- Personal, social, and emotional development.

When children and students with social-communication difficulties are still experiencing gaps in these areas, there is a need to carry on prioritising the learning that would usually occur in pre-school. This may continue throughout their school years, or for as long as it is relevant to their developmental reality. Some of these learners for whom an early-years approach would still be relevant may be young adults in college settings, but the gap between their chronological and developmental age still needs to be acknowledged. These early skills can be taught creatively using materials that would not look out of place within Post-16 learning, while satisfying the demands of developmentally pertinent learning. It is the rationale of an early-years teaching approach that is most important, and we need to be clear about this, to avoid it being dismissed under the assumption that learners older than 5 years of age are being treated like infants or toddlers (read more on developmental pertinence in Chapter 11).

Failing to recognise that teaching these crucial early skills should be a priority for learners with social-communication difficulties – regardless of the student's age – has quite the opposite effect and is, in fact, the greatest failure that can happen in the name of education. Moreover, for children/adults with complex needs or severe learning disabilities, this learning may need to remain a central part of their curriculum/care throughout their entire life, to ensure the social bridge from social isolation to social inclusion is being maintained.

Further challenges must be considered, as mentioned earlier, as some pupils may have what is referred to as a spiky profile (Rees, 2017), meaning that they may have strengths in some areas and limited or minimal abilities in others. For pupils with autism, continued access to an early development social-communication curriculum remains relevant, regardless of their age or cognitive abilities in other, more academic subject areas. Opportunities for social-communication teaching would need to remain the priority within all the subjects, appreciating that 'individuals construct their own world, but they do so within a social context of shared meanings' (Kelly, 2009, p. 53) in authentic social situations.

> Therefore, optimal conditions for teaching need to be supported by both curriculum and pedagogy, always keeping in mind the perspectives of learners learning.
>
> *'All that one can do is to arrange the conditions that might enable people to learn'.*
> *(Sotto, 2007, p. 31)*
>
> This quote encapsulates well the teaching/learning camp into which Intensive Interaction falls. Intensive Interaction is a developmental approach. This means that the learner is at the centre of the learning process, operating as an active participant, fully engaged in the teaching process and the processes of their own development.

## What is learning?

Human beings are born with very little knowledge. The brain, however, is hot-wired for developing and shaping neural links through human connections: 'Relationships and neural linkages together shape the mind. It is more than the sum of its parts; this is the essence of emergence' (Siegel, 2012, p. 3).

Learning therefore starts from day one: not in a low-arousal classroom environment or sitting still giving attention and listening to the teacher, not working on particular objectives assessed on a regular basis. . . . Teaching babies takes place within regular, frequent repetitions of pleasurable activities which are developmentally pertinent and intrinsically motivating. In fact, when it comes to this early learning, we tend not to think about 'teaching' babies. If babies are placed in the right environment, with loving caregivers who tune in to them and are responsive, then a baby's development will follow its course. The learning which takes place in the first three years of life is immense, complex, and multi-faceted. The FoCs lists provide a useful descriptive of the learning, but it is just that: a mere description of the observable outcomes.

The actual learning taking place is the development of neural links and neural connections. And whilst a person's brain may be wired differently or may be impaired due to a genetic condition or brain damage, establishment of synaptic connections is dictated by both genes and experiences. Or, as Siegel puts it:

*experience shape(s) the activity of the brain and the strength of neuronal connections through life, experience in early life may be especially crucial in organizing the way the basic regulatory structures of the brain develop.*

(2012, p. 22)

Whilst the first three years of life are crucial for children's development, findings on the studies of neuroplasticity indicate that the brain is open to further development throughout the lifespan, through a process called epigenesis (Siegel, 2012; Lussier, Islam and Kobor, 2018). Genes provide only a blueprint requiring certain experiences for gene expressions to occur. In other words, these potential epigenetic changes can occur as the result of experiences which modify the structural connections of the brain.

## Social-constructivist approach

Understanding how the brain develops and its capacity to rewire or create new neural connections throughout the lifespan emphasises further the crucial role of intersubjectivity in communication learning and development. By its very nature, this learning is a social activity relying on interpersonal interactions and relationships (Rogoff, 1992; Newson and Newson, 1975; Bateman and Church, 2017).

Communication learning and the development of the FoCs is a dyadic process enabling a set of internal processes of self-construction (Rushton, Juola-Rushton and Larkin, 2010). The process taking place is what Rogoff (1992) beautifully refers to in the title of her book as an 'Apprenticeship in Thinking', facilitating a shared focus and purpose. Learning therefore is not driven by the teacher but occurs in the cognitive zone in which children's learning and development is scaffolded by the teacher who recognises teachable moments when they present themselves (Bruner, 1983; Havighurst, 1952; Pestalozzi, 1898). Known as the child's zone of proximal development (ZPD – Vygotsky, 1978), this is discussed further later. Spontaneous, child-initiated social interactions activate cognitive processes at a neural level. Experiential learning '*enhances the creation of new neurons and the growth of new synaptic connections or the strengthening of existing synapses. This experience-dependent brain growth and differentiation is this referred to as an "activity-dependent" process*' (Siegel, 2012, p. 23).

> Intensive Interaction therefore adopts a social constructivist approach to social-communication development. It fully appreciates the developmental reality of children's learning and their need to construct their own understanding and knowledge of the world by experiencing authentic interactions and reflecting on those experiences (Honebein, 1996).

## Play-based approach and Intensive Interaction

Attempting to teach children with social-communication difficulties the very skills that challenge them can be a daunting prospect. Undeniably, children with social-communication difficulties are more likely to experience stress and anxiety simply by being immersed in social situations in which they need to navigate on an emotional, physiological, and psychological level. High stress hormone levels and a high level of cortisol can not only become toxic to the brain but prevent a child's development/access to learning, regardless of their cognitive abilities (Sotto, 2007; Zeedyk, 2012; Fuld, 2018). The learning environment must therefore be as stress-free as possible. Research demonstrates that developmentally appropriate play with a more knowledgeable person is the best vehicle to promote the social, emotional, cognitive, physical, and self-regulation skills that contribute to executive function and the development of the social brain. Far from being frivolous, play offers the ideal structure for emotional and psychological development within pleasurable and nurturing relationships which are needed for children to thrive (Yogman et al., 2016).

Once again, the EYFS offers a wealth of information on play and describes a play-based approach as one in which the emphasis is on the process of learning rather than the content.

> *The problem is to find a way of teaching that does not inhibit motivation; and second, to find a way of teaching that is in line with the motivation already present in learners.*
>
> (Sotto, 2007, p. 28)

Intensive Interaction is very much a play-based approach, focusing first and foremost on building a relationship. Getting to know the learner enables the practitioner to tune in on an emotional and psychological level, reading the learner's cues moment by moment and responding accordingly whilst supporting the learner to remain within their range of healthy arousal levels through the process of co-regulation. By joining in and responding in ways which are intrinsically motivating, the learner is therefore actively taking part in the activity and rehearsing the very skills and abilities that are otherwise challenging to them.

Play offers opportunities for adults to scaffold and promote skills not via passive rote-learning (see Chapter 9). This creates learning situations that are intrinsically rewarding, supportive and realistic; all the while facilitating social-communication learning to take place in a safe and stress-free environment.

## The zone of proximal development

Another very useful way of thinking about curriculum, teaching and learning is to look at the Russian educational thinker Lev Vygotsky. Vygotsky's model of learning and development provides a framework to support realistic teaching and learning within a social constructivist approach. He defines the zone of proximal development as:

*the distance between the actual developmental level as determined by independent problem solving and the level of potential development as determined through problem-solving under adult guidance or in collaboration with more capable peers.*

(1978, p. 86)

In a sense, the ZPD focuses on future development in an indirect way. Not through targeted, adult-directed action but rather by building on the learner's intrinsic motivation and activating conscious mental processes through the process of scaffolding (Bruner, 1983). The Intensive Interaction practitioner therefore acts as the enabler for activating the mental processes which are essential for learning to occur. The teaching process in this model is seen as a collaborative act in which both pupil and practitioner need to engage to create joint meaning (Silalahi, 2019).

Within this framework, outcomes do not occur in a linear tidy fashion, and it may be difficult if not impossible to predict what they will be. In other words, the outcomes of Intensive Interaction activities are by their very nature non-linear (Hewett, 2012b). And whilst the FoCs are a useful description of the learning outcomes, it is imperative to refrain from targeting specific aspects within the interactions. The issue with targets and objectives is their pervasive impact on practice in a counter-productive way (see Chapters 13 and 14 to read more on target setting/EHC Plans).

> ZPD supports a cognitive development theory, as Vygotsky himself stated that 'The concept does not emerge in the child's mind like a pea in a sack'
>
> (Vygotsky, 1987, p. 224).

## Process-central and emergent outcomes

Planning by targets does not allow for the learning outcomes of the FoCs. Furthermore, a target is 'fundamentally behavioural, linear, instrumental and leads to a loss, rather than an enhancement of freedom for both teacher and pupil' (Kelly, 2009, p. 71). An objective/target-driven approach to the curriculum is at risk of teaching passive recipients and of denying individual freedom (Kelly, 2009).

To set out how to teach, one must understand how people learn:

*to create a carefully structured and inherently interesting learning situation, the focus is on the learners. And the effect of such a shift is to lift a burden from teachers, and to give learners a chance to do some learning.*

(Sotto, 2007, p. 32)

# Teaching and learning approach

With Intensive Interaction, practitioners meet the person where they are at developmentally, regardless of their chronological age. This is achieved by tuning in moment by moment to the learner, to make sure their needs are being met and all teachable moments are seized. By doing so, not only is the developmental reality of the learner being taken into consideration, it also allows for another crucial aspect: learners do not operate on a single level throughout the day; they are likely to move up and down what is traditionally referred to as 'the developmental ladder' (Fischer and Daley, 2006), which will affect their learning style.

Intensive Interaction is a process-central approach, in which the 'outcomes gradually emerge over time, as a result of the rolling, cumulative, generative process of frequent, regular, repetitive activities of Intensive Interaction' (Hewett, 2012b, p. 192). The emphasis is on offering regular opportunities for FoCs moments to occur, for the child to keep on rehearsing and strengthening their attainment in these areas. Hence a process-central model is key, with emergent outcomes arising over time through the frequent repetition of activities (ibid.) in which connecting and bonding are at the core of the process.

A process-central approach therefore does not follow a linear progression but rather a spiral model, implying 'a pattern of progress or moving forward positively' (ibid., p. 150; recording Intensive Interaction outcomes are explained further in Chapter 14).

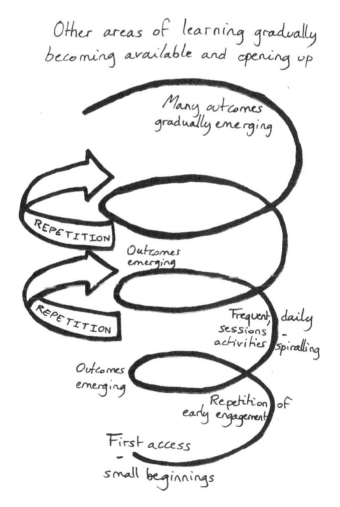

**Figure 4.1** The 'spiral' of progress and development.

The first outcome of an Intensive Interaction activity is to activate the process by enabling the learner to initiate. They therefore learn that they can impact the world around them; that they have a voice and are being listened to. The spiral approach enables the learners to build on and rehearse the FoCs as much and as often as they need to, increasing the level of depth and complexity of their attainment in these areas. The key element for this model to be effective is the communicative partner who facilitates the process. In our terms, the communicative partner is an Intensive Interaction Practitioner.

### The Intensive Interaction Classroom Practitioner

The Intensive Interaction Classroom Practitioner can be defined as any of the adults:

- Working in a classroom setting: teaching assistants, teachers, therapists, etc.
- Who acknowledges the importance of learning the FoCs.
- Who fully appreciates what Intensive Interaction means: that they are the one adapting their style to create a social bridge and meet the learner at their level.
- Who understands the importance of offering an optimal environment for children's development.
- Conscious that their interactive style is key in children's well-being and access to learning.
- Who reflects on good practice and fully appreciates their duty of care to speak up, question, and potentially challenge other colleagues' practice.
- Who appreciates that their emotional state will directly affect the learners and are aware of their responsibility with regards to their own emotional intelligence, including:
  - Being able to convey to the learner that they care.
  - Being able to help themselves by being aware that emotions are contagious.
  - Tuning in and being present, creating a safe and grounding presence.
  - Showing that they care through empathic concern, always striving to listen, read, and hear the person's cues – either verbal or non-verbal.

The role of the Intensive Interaction Classroom Practitioner is central to the learning process: supporting, encouraging, and extending the child's own active search for understanding. There are shared responsibilities in achieving this model at an individual level but also at an organisational level. It is the duty of the school to support, equip, and enhance staff to embody these values (see Chapter 12).

# Concluding remarks

Intensive Interaction practitioners are, in a sense, the most essential piece of educational equipment that there is in a classroom! Teaching starts first and foremost with empathetic and tuned-in individuals who appreciate and celebrate the uniqueness of each pupil and create a safe and intrinsically motivating environment for learning to occur.

# References

Bateman, A. and Church, A. (2017). 'Children's knowledge-in-interaction: An introduction'. In: A. Bateman and A. Church, eds., *Children's Knowledge-in-Interaction*. New York, NY: Springer, pp. 1–11.

Bronfenbrenner, U. (1979). *The Ecology of Human Development: Experiments by Nature and Design*. Cambridge, MA: Harvard University Press.

Bruner, J. (1983). *Child's Talk: Learning to Use Language*. New York: Oxford University Press.

Department for Children, Schools and Families, (2008). *Statutory Framework for the Early Years Foundation Stage*. Available at: https://dera.ioe.ac.uk/6413/7/statutory-framework_Redacted.pdf [Accessed 26 November 2020].

Department for Education, (2014). *The National Curriculum in England Framework Document*. Available at: https://assets.publishing.service.gov.uk/government/uploads/system/uploads/attachment_data/file/381344/Master_final_national_curriculum_28_Nov.pdf [Accessed 26 November 2020].

Department for Education, (2015). *Special Educational Needs and Disability Code of Practice: 0 to 25 Years*. Available at: https://assets.publishing.service.gov.uk/government/uploads/system/uploads/attachment_data/file/398815/SEND_Code_of_Practice_January_2015.pdf [Accessed 26 November 2020].

Department for Education, (2017). *Statutory Framework for the Early Years Foundation Stage*. Available at: https://assets.publishing.service.gov.uk/government/uploads/system/uploads/attachment_data/file/596629/EYFS_STATUTORY_FRAMEWORK_2017.pdf [Accessed 26 November 2020].

Devouche, E. and Gratier, M. (2019). 'The beginning of parent-infant communication'. In: G. Apter, E. Devouche and M. Gratier, eds., *Early Interaction and Developmental Psychopathology*. Cham: Springer. Available at: https://doi.org/10.1007/978-3-030-04769-6_2 [Accessed 26 November 2020].

Fischer, K. W. and Daley, S. (2006). 'Connecting cognitive science and neuroscience to education: Potentials and pitfalls in inferring executive processes'. In: L. Meltser, ed., *Understanding Executive Function: Implications and Opportunities for the Classroom*. New York: Guilford Press.

Fuld, S. (2018). Autism Spectrum Disorder: The impact of stressful and traumatic life events and implications for clinical practice. *Clinical Social Work Journal*, 46(3), pp. 210–219.

Goleman, D. (1995). *Emotional Intelligence: Why It Can Matter More Than IQ*. New York: Bantam Books.

Havighurst, R. J. (1952). *Human Development and Education*. New York: Longman.

Hewett, D. (2012a). 'Blind frogs: The nature of human communication and Intensive Interaction'. In: D. Hewett, ed., *Intensive Interaction: Theoretical Perspectives*. London: Sage Publications, pp. 4–21.

Hewett, D. (2012b). 'What is Intensive Interaction? Curriculum, process and approach'. In: D. Hewett, ed., *Intensive Interaction: Theoretical Perspectives*. London: Sage Publications, pp. 137–154.

Honebein, P. (1996). 'Seven Goals for the design of constructivist learning environments'. In: Wilson, B., ed., *Constructivist Learning Environments*. New York: Educational Technology Publications.

Kelly, A. V. (2009). *The Curriculum: Theory and Practice*. 6th ed. London: Sage Publications.

Kentli, D. (2009). Comparison of hidden curriculum theories. *European Journal of Educational Studies*, 1(2), pp. 83–88.

Lussier, A. A., Islam, S. A. and Kobor, M. S. (2018). 'Epigenetics and genetics of development'. In: R. Gibb and B. Kolb, eds., *The Neurobiology of Brain and Behavioral Development*. Oxford: Elsevier.

Newson, J. and Newson, E. (1975). Intersubjectivity and the transmission of culture: On the social origins of symbolic functioning. *Bulletin of the British Psychological Society*, 28, pp. 437–446.

Pestalozzi, J. H. (1898). *Comment Gertrude Instruit Ses Enfants*. Paris: Lib C. Delagrave.

Rees, K. (2017). Models of disability and the categorisation of children with severe and profound learning difficulties: Informing educational approaches based on an understanding of individual needs. *Educational and Child Psychology*, 34(4), pp. 30–39.

Rogoff, B. (1992). *Apprenticeship in Thinking*. New York: Oxford University Press.

Rushton, S., Juola-Rushton, A. and Larkin, E. (2010). Neuroscience, play and early childhood education: Connections, implications and assessment. *Early Childhood Education Journal*, 37(5), pp. 351–361.

Siegel, D. (2012). *The Developing Mind*. 2nd ed. New York: Guilford Press.

Silalahi, R. (2019). Understanding Vygotsky's zone of proximal development for learning. *Polyglot: Jurnal Ilmiah*, 15(2), pp. 169–186.

Sotto, E. (2007). *When Teaching Becomes Learning*. 2nd ed. London: Continuum International Publishing Group.

Standards and Testing Agency, (2020). *The Engagement Model Guidance for Maintained Schools, Academies (Including Free Schools) and Local Authorities*. Available at: www.evidenceforlearning.net/wp-content/uploads/2020/06/The_engagement_model_guidance_for_maintained_schools_academies_free_schools_and_local_authorities.pdf [Accessed 12 February 2020].

Tharp, R. and Gallimore, R. (1988). *Rousing Minds to Life: Teaching, Learning, and Schooling in Social Context*. Cambridge: Cambridge University Press.

Vygotsky, L. S. (1978). *Mind in Society: The Development of Higher Psychological Processes*. Cambridge, MA: Harvard University Press.

Vygotsky, L. S. (1987). 'The development of scientific concepts in childhood'. In: R. W. Rieber and A. S. Carton, eds., *Collected Works of L. S. Vygotsky: Vol. I. Problems of General Psychology*. New York: Plenum, pp. 167–241.

Yogman, M., Garner, A., Hutchinson, J., Hirsh-Pasek, K. and Michnick Golinkoff, R. (2016). The power of play: A pediatric role in enhancing development in young children. *American Academy of Pediatrics*, 142(3), pp. 1–16.

Zeedyk, M. S. (2012). 'Wired for communication: How the neuroscience of infancy helps in understanding the effectiveness of intensive interaction'. In: D. Hewett, ed., *Intensive Interaction: Theoretical Perspectives*. London: Sage Publications, pp. 55–71.

# 5. My journey to Intensive Interaction in the Early Years Foundation Stage

*Rhianne Richards*

As an early-years teacher working in an environment with changing expectations of the Early Years Foundation Stage (EYFS) curriculum (Department for Education -DfE, 2017), it can be challenging to support children with special educational needs and/or disabilities (SEND). With that in mind, I had to find ways to adapt my teaching to ensure my pupils were making progress, whilst also being aware of the impact on children's well-being when faced with substantial adult-led learning.

Pritchard (2014, p. 85) notes that stress causes anxiety and if children become anxious about school, then they will *'fail to function effectively'*. Anxiety is more likely to arise in learning situations in which children do not have control. This highlights the importance of the child-led agenda and play in EYFS provision for children to learn effectively. We know this empowers children because it gives them control, allowing them to set goals and choose who they play with. EYFS settings therefore play a vital role in providing a child with the ability to take control of their learning and enrich a child's life skills. This is something a child with SEND may not have experienced before in the home due to stress, anxiety, or lack of independence. In this way, the principles of Intensive Interaction fitted perfectly into supporting this concept, and I began my journey implementing this into my classroom. This chapter will look specifically at embedding Intensive Interaction in early-years settings, considering the Early Years Foundation Stages and Curriculum.

The core principles of Intensive Interaction are highly compatible with the play-based approach that underpins early-years education. This method of teaching and facilitating communication makes Intensive Interaction easily accessible for EYFS practitioners. I started to explore the relationship between 'playing to learn' and 'learning to play' for children with SEND. Most children in the EYFS can independently play and learn with an enabling environment and adults facilitating opportunities to extend and support learning situations. However, many children with complex needs require additional support to learn how to play. The Fundamentals of Communication (FoCs – Nind and Hewett, 2001) facilitate these early play skills, such as attention and listening, turn-taking, learning to do sequences of activity with another person, and self-regulation. I am exceptionally proud of the progress my EYFS class made after implementing Intensive Interaction, and it has had a positive impact on my teaching and professional development. I hope to offer some practical ideas to support other EYFS practitioners in this chapter and inspire others to implement the wonders of Intensive Interaction.

DOI: 10.4324/9781003170839-5

## The EYFS framework and Intensive Interaction

The early years curriculum is a statutory framework based on the central importance of the 'unique child' having opportunities to interact in 'positive relationships' and 'enabling environments' (DfE, 2017). Using this framework, it proved easy to weave the principles of Intensive Interaction into our practice as EYFS practitioners. The framework emphasises that *'Every child is a unique child, who is constantly learning and can be resilient, capable, confident and self-assured'*. The Fundamentals of Communication 2 (FoCs 2 – Hewett, 2018, see also Chapter 3) on emotional learning are pertinent here; particularly supporting children with SEND to build their sense of self and self-esteem. The role of the responsive adult is vital in nurturing this confidence and resilience. This also connects the next phrase whereby *'Children learn to be strong and independent through positive relationships'*. It highlights the importance of attachment, attunement, and supporting self-security, which can be achieved through Intensive Interaction.

---

### EYFS framework – characteristics of effective learning

- Playing and exploring.
- Active learning.
- Creating and thinking critically.

---

## Integrating Intensive Interaction into the EYFS curriculum

The EYFS framework encompasses the Characteristics of Effective Learning (CoEL), which holds three key interlinking features about how children learn: *'It is about becoming an independent thinker and learner who is able to make decisions and choices and interpret their ideas and solve problems'* (Chilvers, 2013, p. 4). The first characteristic, playing and exploring, looks at a child's levels of engagement. When we consider engagement levels, it is more than a child's listening and attention; it is their awareness of others and how they make sense of the world around them and interact with it. Children with SEND may need more support to experience positive social and emotional engagement.

Our social and emotional engagement levels are expressed predominantly through our body language. Intensive Interaction creates an opportunity to support levels of engagement by focusing on tuning in and understanding gestures, which supports children with SEND to integrate and participate. In addition, Intensive Interaction also gives a practitioner the tools to begin to understand a child's subtle communicative gestures – for example, recognising if a child's stimming is a sign of distress or a calming measure – and further support their engagement with appropriate action. Secondly, active learning considers a child's motivation, such as their involvement, concentration, and learning resilience. Similarly, Intensive Interaction is about learning and using language that is meaningful for the child to communicate and build positive relationships.

Intensive Interaction allows children to become active learners by taking risks with their social-communication and building resilience in these situations. Finally, the third characteristic, creating and thinking critically, explores a child's creativity, ideas, and individuality. Intensive Interaction allows play experimentation to take place through child-led communication. It gives a child the opportunity to be curious at a level they can process and builds their confidence through familiarity with these interactions.

The EYFS curriculum then connects the CoEL, the 'how', to begin to look specifically at 'what' children learn. This is broken down initially into three prime areas. Firstly, the growth of a child's personal, social, and emotional development (PSED), which is fundamental to the early years curriculum and essential to ensure children are ready to learn. Children with SEND encounter further barriers to their learning and development; for example, they may find it challenging to emotionally regulate themselves and have high arousal levels that are easily overstimulated. Further to this, a child with complex needs may find it difficult to build relationships with others or understand that they can gain positive and pleasurable experiences from interactions.

Recognising these barriers, Intensive Interaction provides a way to support children with SEND and improve their personal, social, and emotional development. Whilst applying the practice and principles of Intensive Interaction, I found children in my class gained confidence with this child-led focus and made significant progress in the area of PSED.

## Case studies in the EYFS classroom

> Charlotte has a dual diagnosis of autism and a global development delay. She had previously displayed little interest in adults and would often move away if they came into her personal space. After two academic terms of embedding Intensive Interaction, we noticed that she not only tolerated adults in her space, but she began to actively seek them out to interact with them. Her mother also began to notice changes at home. Charlotte became more affectionate and desired her mother's attention rather than evading all interaction opportunities.
>
> Jo has a visual impairment and global development delay. She finds interacting with adults overwhelming and is extremely sensitive to noise. Staff have started positive interactions with her by blowing softly on her hand when she placed it near their face. Slowly she is beginning to show improvements in her FoC skills, enjoying being with others and learning to do sequences of activity with another person. She shows pleasure in this interaction by smiling and repeating the action.
>
> David has social-communication difficulties and sensory-processing difficulties. He demonstrates high levels of arousal and becomes easily overstimulated during activities, causing him to throw things,

> bite himself, or seek movement through his arms by flapping. He responds well to an adult's ability to tune into his play and interacting in order to calm his play. Joining in with his actions and providing calmer alternatives supports him to self-regulate better. For example, if he becomes overstimulated during water play, staff copy his actions or vocalisations in a calmer and quieter way that he in turn responds to.

The next prime area of EYFS curriculum is communication and language development, which is broken down into three key areas: attention and listening, understanding, and speaking. Children with SEND can find it difficult to meet the age-related expectations, and it can be challenging for EYFS practitioners to evidence progress made using the EYFS development framework. By understanding and appreciating the importance of the FoCs and the way in which children develop, children with SEND are able to make progress with their social-communication skills. When an adult applies techniques such as tuning in, pausing, observing, and waiting, it allows the child to process and lead interactions, which supports their attention and listening. Responding in a calm way and following the child's lead creates predictability and supports their understanding. Furthermore, responding to their vocalisations allows the child to begin to vocalise meaningfully and supports the development of early speech.

> Jenna has profound and multiple learning difficulties. Through Intensive Interaction, Jenna found her voice at school. Adults had rarely heard her babble or vocalise beforehand. As her confidence to vocalise grew using Intensive Interaction, Jenna developed her phatic communication (Malinowski, 1923). One year on, she regularly vocalises to share her feelings and thoughts, frequently engaging in her own chit-chat with adults in the room to express herself throughout the day. Jenna understands communication is two-way communication now and is noticeably happier. The importance of these small-talk conversations to build relationships – something we often take for granted – must therefore never be underestimated.

The final prime area of the EYFS is physical development. Children in my EYFS classroom are usually also known to physiotherapy and occupational therapy services with outlined goals and therapy programmes to follow. Children with complex medical needs sometimes have negative experiences of professionals from hospital or clinic visits and can as a result be wary of therapists and other adults. I ensured that any therapists coming into my EYFS classroom understood the principles of Intensive Interaction and followed the approach to support the children. We moved towards a way therapy could become child-led, which gave children independence and control in the situation. With a focus on the FoCs and building these skills, children progressed with their concentration to tasks, learned to share their personal space and enjoyed being with another person.

> Alex has four-limb cerebral palsy. He is very anxious around adults and would often resist physiotherapy time by stiffening his limbs, crying, and pushing adults away. Alex associated physiotherapy with pain and something 'done to' him, rather than having any ownership of the situation. Through Intensive Interaction, he built positive and trusting relationships with adults, and this in turn made physiotherapy time easier. Additionally, we used Intensive Interaction techniques to make physiotherapy child-led; if Alex moved his arm out, for example, we would imitate this and respond with an added physiotherapy stretch, which he would often try to copy.
>
> Jamila has profound and multiple learning difficulties with complex medical needs. We looked to use Intensive Interaction to primarily improve her communication, but as a result, we also found this development improved physical development too. Jamila showed greater awareness and engagement with adults, her sitting posture improved, and she gained awareness of her right hand to play.

## Creating a responsive EYFS environment

Early-years settings are busy environments – enriched with colours, toys, noise, bustling learning situations – which creates a sensory overload for some children. It is noted that children with SEND learn better in quieter and decluttered environments. This makes navigating an EYFS setting difficult for some children. One of the key learning points for my classroom was to consider noise levels; we often like music playing, loud and exciting toys, with a buzz of adults and children talking. Whilst implementing an Intensive Interaction approach, I found the best interactions took place where children with SEND are not distracted by noise. By turning off the music in the room and ensuring all staff were talking in a quiet and soft voice, the quality of interactions with children improved. Children appeared calmer and more focused, and importantly it gave children opportunities to vocalise and communicate better. I started to pick up and tune into small vocalisations that had not previously been noticeable, such as small breathing sounds.

Whilst it is important to consider adapting the environment to support children with special educational needs, Intensive Interaction does not need to take place in a clinical blank space. It is essential to tune in and create opportunities to interact in the environment. When applying Intensive Interaction to the EYFS classroom, I found it was not necessary to remove all the activities on offer despite initial worries that children would become fixated on certain objects. By contrast, however, I discovered that toys could easily be used as tools to create quality interaction and play opportunities.

> Zainab has a dual diagnosis of autism and a global development delay. She is pre-verbal, enjoys building towers and structures with blocks, and engages repetitively with this activity for long periods. She finds adult-led activities difficult to engage with and will often move away if an adult

comes into her play space. Through Intensive Interaction, we found a way of tuning into her play by handing her the bricks to build with. By interacting this way, we were playing on her terms and her 'rules', and she allowed us to play alongside her and tolerated us in her space. This child-led play then developed further into a game of passing the bricks and adding a noise during this interaction. This allowed for a 'pause and wait' moment, extending the communication and bringing some focus to the adult interacting. Zainab began to anticipate this game, watching the adult with interest and giving her first moments of eye contact. Zainab showed enjoyment from this interaction, smiling and willing for it to continue with vocalisations. By tuning in to Zainab's play, she began to enjoy interactions with adults. This later led to Zainab initiating communication with adults to request, rather than avoid them.

Hakim has a diagnosis of autism. He has lots of spontaneous language, which has not yet developed functionally. Hakim loves playing with balls, particularly rolling and throwing them. He is a busy and active boy, which became a barrier to interactions. It is difficult to get his attention for more than a few moments, and he is easily distracted. By using his interest in balls, adults were able to copy his actions; for example, rolling a ball down a large slide and following his lead in play. Hakim began to notice this interaction, allowing adults to add a 'pause and wait' after rolling the ball. Slowly he began to anticipate the game and invite them to play along by picking up the ball and placing it in the adult's hand to repeat. It is important to note that this interaction did not take place instantaneously; it took Hakim many weeks of short bursts of Intensive Interaction input or moments to begin to notice adults. It demonstrates the need to persevere with this approach in order to see the results.

Using resources as tools to support interaction works well with some children; however, it is important to ensure that the resource does not become a barrier. Ellie has profound and multiple learning difficulties. She enjoys playing with cause-and-effect toys when lying on the floor and will repetitively play with these toys to create sounds. However, in this case, the toys became a barrier for Intensive Interaction to take place, as she would focus her attention only on the toy. It was important not to force interaction with Ellie by immediately removing the toy and expecting her to interact with the adult instead. By lying beside Ellie and allowing time for her to notice an adult, her attention shifted to the adult, who became the exciting focus instead of the toy.

## The role of the reflective adult

Implementing Intensive Interaction into our EYFS setting has improved the role and practice of all adults working in the setting. Staff were struck with the simplicity of the approach and its effectiveness to support children with complex needs. The changes were subtle but the impact on the children's development was significant. Intensive Interaction fits in perfectly with early-years practice, but the reflection brought about from Intensive Interaction helps get it just right for those children who are more difficult to reach or have social-communication difficulties.

We started to focus on the importance of the FoCs and the techniques, particularly tuning in and pausing/waiting to allow more processing time. We slowed down with both our interactions and the daily timetable, and as a result, staff were calmer, more relaxed, and enjoyed themselves, which is essential to apply Intensive Interaction effectively. It is easy to become overwhelmed with the increasing paperwork and target setting in EYFS provision with many types of SEND interventions, but I felt Intensive Interaction simplified the workload with significant changes noted for our children's development.

## Adult to child ratios

Whilst implementing Intensive Interaction in our pilot year, we found that the best interactions took place with a higher adult ratio. This understandably can be difficult at times in a busy school setting, but we planned times to ensure children could receive quality interaction time. For example, splitting a group for garden play or time in the sensory room in order to quieten the classroom environment. As Intensive Interaction embedded itself into the staff's everyday practice, we began to take small and frequent opportunities throughout the day to carry it out.

## Positioning of the adult

Adults need to be at the child's level at all times in order to create the best opportunities to interact. In an EYFS setting this means sitting on carpets and lying down sometimes in order to be close for face-to-face interactions. By embracing the strategies of Intensive Interaction as a team and understanding the rationale behind it, adults felt comfortable doing this knowing it was important (including the moment an Ofsted inspector came into my classroom with all EYFS practitioners lying on the carpet with the children and vocalising!).

## The reflective practitioner

A key element to the success of implementing Intensive Interaction and sustaining high-quality practice was being a reflective practitioner. Staff were given many opportunities throughout the pilot year and beyond this to reflect through video observations, discuss ideas with the team, and make changes to improve interactions. We began with a one-day Intensive Interaction training course from the Institute, which was followed up with visits from Amandine Mourière to support and coach staff in the adoption of Intensive Interaction practice and techniques.

In our pilot year, we picked four children only to create a clear focus on gaining experience with this approach and finding ways to track this effectively. Initially staff had to plan times in the day that were set aside to carry out Intensive Interaction sessions to ensure we were consistently practising with a clear understanding of the FoCs as the learning outcomes. Early-years practitioners paired with a team partner and took turns to video each other during interactions. They used reflection sheets after interactions to establish what went well, actions copied, and any responses. EYFS staff shared their favourite moments of video interactions in staff meetings regularly, and we celebrated the progression of staff and children.

# Recording

## Reflection sheet example from an early-years practitioner

| Recording Sheet: Intensive Interaction ||||||
|---|---|---|---|---|---|
| **Name:** Charlotte ||||||
| **Date** 31.01.20 | **Time** 10.30 | **Venue** EYFS specialist nursery || **Your name** Rhianne ||
| Encounter ☑ | Awareness ☑ | Attention & Response ☑ | Engagement ☑ | Participation ☑ | Involvement ☑ |
| **Context/where** <br> In the classroom, free play, <br> Adult sat on carpet at child's eye level, child standing up ||||||
| **What happened in interaction?** <br> Charlotte was playing with a shaker instrument. She was holding it above her head and then dropping it to the ground, listening to the sound and making 'ehh' vocalisations. Adult joined game by finding occasions to pick up shaker and hand to Charlotte to repeat action. Charlotte allowed adult to play along with this game to her 'rules'. Adult then took moment to have a turn raising shaker and dropping to floor. Gradually the adult increased the time she held the shaker in the air to build anticipation and adding pause/wait. Charlotte looked towards adult on several occasions smiling and anticipating the game. Charlotte then picked up the shaker and offered it to the adult to repeat on one occasion. ||||||
| **What actions did the adult respond to?** <br> Ehh sounds <br> Props used and movements imitated - dropping the shaker. ||||||
| **How did client respond?** <br> Charlotte allowed adult in her space and allowed adult to touch the shaker (focus object). <br> Charlotte noticed the adult by smiling and watching them join-in with her actions. She paused and interacted with adult by passing her the shaker. Charlotte made 'ehhh' vocalisations when excited. ||||||
| **Significant events** <br> Charlotte showed awareness of the adult. She invited her to play by handing her the shaker, after noticing they were playing the same child-led game. ||||||
| **Evaluation** <br> Charlotte showed preference for particular objects and engaged in II for 10 minutes. She could re-engage with adult after another child took the shaker for a moment. She showed good self-regulation skills and quickly refocused after a brief interruption. ||||||

**Table 5.1** Intensive Interaction Recording Sheet.

Staff also wrote any significant events on our monthly tracking sheets so we could track small steps of progress for the child. I found this an exceptionally useful tool as it is often difficult to celebrate these significant developmental milestones for children with SEND within the EYFS development matters framework. These tracking sheets were also shared with parents to celebrate progress. Any initial concerns I had with using this format from the Intensive Interaction Institute were reassured when we had an Ofsted inspection in our pilot year who were equally interested and impressed by this system.

## Tracking sheet example for a child

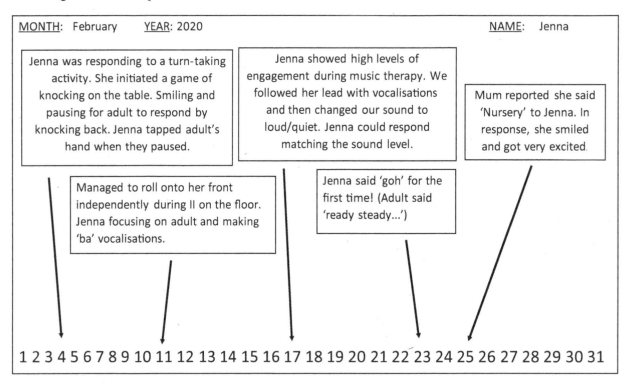

**Figure 5.1** The progress track.

# Concluding remarks

Applying techniques of Intensive Interaction felt intuitive as it fitted in with the principles of good EYFS practice and aligned with the school's ethos. After an academic term of practicing, we rapidly embedded Intensive Interaction into daily practice without having to plan the time to implement specific sessions. A vital part of this was confirming we had a whole-team approach to understanding and believing in the process and the changes we were making. It has taken the pressure off our assessments, and as a result staff are more reflective in ensuring high-quality interactions. Law et al. (2017, p. VI) notes '*The quality of input that children receive is likely to be more important than the quantity*'. Further, EYFS staff have a deeper understanding of the children's early development and ways to support communication for a wide range of children with SEND.

Intensive Interaction can be accessible for any child with SEND in the EYFS, regardless of their individualities. For example, if they are pre-verbal, speaking, visually impaired, hearing impaired, or have profound learning needs or social-communication needs.

I think this is part of the wonder of Intensive Interaction unlike many other interventions. We began to spend noticeably more quality time with the children, and as a result learning became more child-led as we moved away from adult-heavy activities. Children with SEND made exceptional progress in the prime areas of EYFS curriculum through adopting an Intensive Interaction philosophy. Intensive Interaction enabled us to create a socially inclusive EYFS setting; my class could finally socialise at an accessible level where they could process, learn, and respond with their thoughts, ideas, and feelings.

# References

Chilvers, D. (2013). *Creating and Thinking Critically*. London: Practical Pre-School Books.

Department for Education, (2017). *Statutory Framework for the Early Years Foundation Stage: Setting the Standards for Learning, Development and Care for Children from Birth to Five*. Available at: https://assets.publishing.service.gov.uk/government/uploads/system/uploads/attachment_data/file/596629/EYFS_STATUTORY_FRAMEWORK_2017.pdf [Accessed 25 February 2021].

Hewett, D. (2018). 'Preparing for intensive interaction'. In: D. Hewett, ed., *The Intensive Interaction Handbook*, 2nd ed. London: Sage Publications, pp. 25–39.

Law, J., Charlton, J., Dockrell, J., Gascoigne, M., McKean, C. and Theakston, A. (2017). *Early Language Development: Needs, Provision, and Intervention for Preschool Children from Socio-Economically Disadvantaged Backgrounds*. London: Education Endowment Foundation.

Malinowski, B. (1923). 'The problem of meaning in primitive languages'. In: K. C. Ogden and I. A. Richards, eds., *The Meaning of Meaning: A Study of the Influence of Language Upon Thought and of the Science of Symbolism*, Supplement 1, 4th ed., revised 1936. London: Kegan Paul, Trench, Trubner.

Nind, M. and Hewett, D. (2001). *A Practical Guide to Intensive Interaction*. Kidderminster: British Institute of Learning Disabilities.

Pritchard, A. (2014). *Ways of Learning*. 2nd ed. London: Routledge.

# 6. Developing a whole-school approach to using Intensive Interaction to promote social communication and well-being

*Debbie Stagg*

In 2012, I completed the Intensive Interaction Coordinator Course, trained and mentored in person by Dave Hewett. We were the third cohort of trainees, and the group was a diverse mix of colleagues from health, social care, education, and also a parent. This made for an extraordinarily rich experience, with opportunities to see how Intensive Interaction could be used successfully and joyfully with people of all ages and needs. We met regularly for 3 days every half-term over 18 months and followed each other's journeys as we all developed in confidence and expertise. At the course, away from our day jobs, we could be totally immersed in Intensive Interaction. These were precious times during which we developed our understanding of Intensive Interaction theory and practice, shared our successes and difficulties with embedding Intensive Interaction throughout our schools and workplaces, and learned from one another through sharing and evaluating our Intensive Interaction videos. It was a life-changing experience and a real joy to walk into those rooms knowing that I was part of something much bigger than me and to be with people who really understood the vital role played by Intensive Interaction in the lives of people learning to become social communicators.

Part of the course involved writing a proposal of how we would implement and develop Intensive Interaction in our workplace. This was daunting, especially when it meant leaving our cosy, supportive group of fellow Intensive Interaction Coordinators and returning to the 'real' world with all the daily pressures on time and staff. But the training gave me the tools and passion to put this into action, and I was determined to put Intensive Interaction in its rightful, central place within each child's learning at my school. This chapter is a reflection upon how I went about implementing this strategy to develop a whole-school approach to using Intensive Interaction to promote social communication and well-being.

DOI: 10.4324/9781003170839-6

> Freemantles is a Surrey LEA School for children aged 4–19 with autism and complex needs. All the students share a core difficulty around communication and social communication as a part of their autism diagnosis. Our senior leadership management team (SLMT) were aware of Intensive Interaction and its value for our students and had shown their commitment to the approach by giving me time to attend the course and paying for the training. This had been a huge, conscious investment on their part, so I felt under quite a lot of pressure to deliver and make a big difference to justify this funding. But that was OK – I was up for the fight because I believe Intensive Interaction is the best thing in the world!

## The challenge – first steps

Prior to my training I had been working as a Senior Teaching Assistant at the school for many years, so I was well-established and respected by my colleagues. I had trained two mentees as part of the Coordinator's course, so I knew that others shared my enthusiasm and supported me. Despite this, I knew that embedding Intensive Interaction throughout the school would not be easy! Dave had told us to start by involving people who were already interested then gradually work towards engaging people who were more sceptical as things became more established. So, I started to develop my game plan.

I began offering mentee courses to staff and had a great response, especially from the Primary Department. I also invited Sara Moroza-James (the parent from my Intensive Interaction Coordinator's course), to come and speak with our parents, which kick-started some interest in a Parents' Menteeship Course.

I started making Intensive Interaction more visible around the school. Firstly, using simple guerilla tactics, such as sticking the Fundamentals of Communication (FoCs) 1 and 2 (see Chapter 3) all around the school. They were on the back of the toilet doors, displayed in each class and staff room, on windows facing outwards into the playgrounds, incorporated into displays of school values in the reception area. Anywhere and everywhere in fact so that staff would always have them in mind.

After this, I requested meetings with the Senior Leadership Management Team (SLMT) and governors to give feedback on my Intensive Interaction training. The focus of these meetings was to show how the money they had invested in me had been used; so I showed my final project video. This tracked the progress of a young man (Matthew) with whom I had worked throughout the course. I showed the huge progress Matthew had made and explained how Intensive Interaction underpins all learning (Hewett, 2012). My presentation had a big impact, and I started to feel that the SLMT and governors were prepared to put their faith in my abilities to develop Intensive Interaction within the school.

I continued to take every opportunity to spread the word, showing Intensive Interaction videos to staff on INSET days, speaking to anyone who would listen about the power of Intensive Interaction, holding special Intensive

Interaction celebration days where treats were offered in the staffroom in exchange for phatic communication (see Chapters 7 and 11) and, most importantly, leading by example and modelling Intensive Interaction wherever and whenever the opportunity arose. It took more meetings with the SLMT and governors, persistence, justification, and huge determination to change the ethos of the school, but eventually it happened! I did it!

However, running a class full time as well as assuming the role of Intensive Interaction Coordinator became virtually impossible! It was soon decided that my week would be split: half the time in class and the other half bringing Intensive Interaction to the forefront of the school. Having this allocated time made a huge difference in enabling me to embed Intensive Interaction across the school, and I will always be grateful to my Head and SLMT for recognising the value of my Intensive Interaction Coordinator's role.

## What does Intensive Interaction look like throughout the school?

Working as the Intensive Interaction Coordinator throughout the whole school has given me the great opportunity to see the progress, and how the application of Intensive Interaction can look so different as it adapts to the individual students as they move through the school from Early Years to Post-16. Regardless of age or cognitive ability, I have found that Intensive Interaction remains essential learning for all our students as it develops social communication and emotional well-being through non-pressurised, enjoyable, error-free learning. Not surprisingly, Intensive Interaction in Early Years may look different than in Post-16. However, as we will see, the same principles apply.

It is worth considering some key points around implementing Intensive Interaction throughout an all-age school and some of the challenges and advantages this brings. For example, what might an ideal classroom look like, how can Intensive Interaction be incorporated as key learning with all students, and how do we tackle issues such as the relevance of Intensive Interaction with cognitively able students who have language but still struggle with self-regulation or social communication? Some issues that arise as the students get older, such as discussions around the issues of touch and age-appropriateness are examined in detail in Chapter 11, so I will not be covering them here.

## What might an ideal Intensive Interaction–friendly classroom look like?

Freemantles School was built in 2007 for educating children with autism and complex needs. As a purpose-built school, it was designed to offer flexible working spaces. This is perfect for Intensive Interaction, giving plenty of small work areas and cubby holes where scheduled/timetabled Intensive Interaction sessions can happen.

Knowing the individual and how they are on the day, in that moment, can help to determine if a session is likely to be dynamic or reflective. It may then be possible to match the space to the mood. For example, individual work rooms, relaxation areas, sensory rooms, or outside areas may be ideal for more calm, peaceful sessions. More dynamic sessions may take place in a soft play area, playground, trim trail, swing, or swimming pool. In addition to these scheduled sessions, however, it is important to be ready and responsive in the moment and to adapt and respond instantaneously when spontaneous interactions occur. At these times, being totally focused on the child can be enough to form a communication bubble where no one else's noise or activities seem to matter, even in a busy classroom. This means Intensive Interaction can take place 'any time, any place, anywhere'.

## Staff support and development

At the start of the new school year the whole school focuses upon building relationships between new staff, new teams, and new children. To support team working, I go to each class with a blank timetable and ask when they would like me to come and work with the team as a whole, and we review this termly. As the students need Intensive Interaction input throughout the day, every day there is no point in me coming in for brief sessions to build relations and then disappearing till next week! Intensive Interaction must be spontaneous and always available, so I step back and let the staff build and establish relationships.

My priority for new staff is establishing a mentor system. This involves modelling good practice, working alongside them, sharing videos of their Intensive Interaction sessions, books, articles, thoughts, and principles. Videos play a huge role in developing good practice and encouraging self-reflection. Although staff may be wary or embarrassed about watching themselves at first, they soon lose their inhibitions by focusing on the child. Once staff are confident about their practice, I take a step back. As staff become more confident Intensive Interaction practitioners, they take on responsibility for mentoring others. But I always remain available to offer support and brainstorm ideas, run regular updates and training and ensure that Intensive Interaction continues to have a central place within each class and for each student. Regular, ongoing Intensive Interaction training sessions and updates for all staff happen throughout the year. Although it can be challenging to find a convenient time to meet, we often schedule times on Friday afternoons when the children leave early to allow for staff training.

## What does Intensive Interaction look like in Early Years and Reception

The Early Years and Reception classes are where Intensive Interaction learning truly begins, setting the foundations for the rest of the child's school career. Staff in these classes are usually very energetic, agile, dynamic, and able to keep up with some extremely active children! As the Intensive Interaction sessions often involve lively, physical play at this stage, we need to be ready to join in and be on their level – if children are on the floor, we must be there with them and also be ready to jump up again when they do! Our Intensive Interaction mantra for children at this stage is: get down, get dirty!

### Setting a baseline

Our work with Early Years and Reception children starts with observation, finding out their likes and dislikes and setting a baseline for showing progression in communication and social skills. It can be challenging to find time for observation, but they are essential, and it may help to run split-group sessions to free up staff members and book specialist rooms (if needed) in advance. Baseline observation videos showing the child engaging with their special interest are especially helpful (see Appendices 1 and 2). These can then be used in a team meeting to show a child's potential level of engagement and remind people that they need to become as interesting as the special object; then, in time, even more fun than that! Incidentally, there is no need to take a special object away during sessions as it may become the joint focus of the interaction, or the focus may gradually shift away from the object and potentially even be discarded as the interaction and relationship with you grows.

Once a baseline has been carried out, I support staff with completing individual communication assessment sheets and help them decide on the method of record keeping that suits them best, discussing what level of detail they need, and adjusting recording to individual needs. Record keeping is a huge area in itself and is discussed further in Chapter 14.

### Challenges and priorities in Early Years and Reception

The children in Early Years and Reception are emerging communicators at the early stages of communication and social interaction. Some may be finding it difficult to express or indeed even to understand their own wants and needs. You need to allow plenty of processing time (pausing and waiting) at this stage and age. I always explain to staff that although they may feel like they are doing nothing when they are waiting and pausing, this is far from the case. They are in fact providing the children with time for their most important learning and enabling them to file away all the information they need to process.

Building relationships with these early learners is key. It is essential to build trust and convey with our body language that we want to share time together. The student needs to know that they are, at this moment in time, the most enjoyable and meaningful communicator in the room. Convey that you want to listen, that everything they do or say has meaning. My mantra is: 'We are who we are, at this moment in time, so let's learn together to enjoy being together'.

# What does Intensive Interaction look like in the Primary Department?

There will naturally be a huge range of differences between individual children in the Primary Department. However, the learners at this stage are generally still at the beginning of their Intensive Interaction journey and may still have minimum knowledge of the FoCs. They may be starting to enjoy being with another person and sharing mutual enjoyment, building trusting relationships and starting to devise and exchange a repertoire of behaviour and activities with more than one person. The interaction may be the same, but extensions and scenarios may start to be added – the focus is always on the relationship, not so much on the content. 'It's not about the game'!

Individual's anxiety levels during Intensive Interaction may be starting to diminish as the 'game' becomes more predictable and familiar. Everything that happens is still, crucially, underpinning the FoCs, but the children may possibly need to spend less time pausing as they start, through the process of neuroplasticity, developing more established neural pathways. The learner may start initiating more interactions which are longer, more complex, with more people and possibly starting to involve peers (often with support at this stage). The focus is to establish genuine two-way communication and sustain it for longer. Turn-taking sequences are still essential learning at this point, and the child will still need time to rehearse these many, many times over. Sessions may over-run! Try not to stop just because it is playtime. This learning is crucial, central, and must be valued.

## Challenges and priorities in the Primary Department

In the Primary Department, the curriculum continues to include a large element of play-based learning, allowing frequent opportunities for Intensive Interaction. The ethos continues to be 'any time, any place, anywhere'. Children will be progressing at quite different rates, and it is always worth revisiting the previous year's baseline observation with the staff team to discuss and look at all the things that have changed for the individual, which may be subtle. Remember, some children may take longer to show progress than others, but keep going! It is completely worth it, and small changes can make a huge difference for some children. Once the child gets the hang of Intensive Interaction, they may try to initiate more frequently, sometimes right in the middle of a structured lesson! If this causes any concern among the team, discuss the school ethos with them and reassure them that if Intensive Interaction is in the child's Individual Learning Plan (ILP – which it will be) it will still fit in with the curriculum, so carry on and record it!

At this point I must mention briefly the 'curse' of language and other people's expectations. People may have totally different expectations of a child with language regarding their behaviour compared with a pre-verbal child. They may also query why a child needs Intensive Interaction if they can speak. However, as stated earlier, because Intensive Interaction supports communication, social communication, and additionally helps with developing emotional regulation, it remains essential learning for all children with autism regardless of their age or verbal abilities (Mourière, 2018).

If children have speech, you can work with the language that the child offers you. They may well be using vocalisations or words with some meaning and intonation. As always, tune in to the individual, use their vocalisations or words, keep responses minimal so there is less to process, and use intonation and pitch to add interest to the exchange. Even if the meaning does not seem clear, work with them where they are as this can support the development of meaningful speech over time.

At this stage, the learner may be having difficulty with understanding, expressing, and regulating their emotions. Intensive Interaction sessions can offer repeated opportunities to feel the physical sensation of emotions, experience co-regulation with an adult, and work towards self-regulation if they start 'bubbling'. It takes time, huge empathy, and being very tuned in to an individual who may be very volatile in their responses to support this learning. But there is no better way to learn to self-regulate and build trusting relationships than through laughter in an Intensive Interaction session adjusted specifically to meet the individual's needs, exactly where they are.

## What does Intensive Interaction look like in the Secondary Department?

In the Secondary Department, students have access to shared communal areas outside of lesson times. At this stage, these students will have experienced Intensive Interaction for several years, and some will be starting to apply what they have learnt within their safe space with trusted peers (and subtle adult support if required). We have found that Intensive Interaction and Intensive Interaction-style communication with adults – student centred, tuned in, and always nurturing – continues to be an essential part of these students' lives, supporting further development of their social communication skills, emotional regulation, and promoting improved self-awareness and well-being.

I often hear more of the chit-chat and hot air of phatic communication going on between students in the Secondary Department – frequently about computer games or shared special interests. Some students will be using single words, others may even be constructing sentences, but in all cases, they are much more skilled communicators than when they joined the school. The staff continue to support students by helping to structure their conversations, clarifying or repairing miscommunications, and developing or nurturing friendships. Through this supported peer-to-peer communication, students practice turn-taking, listening, and speaking, and their exchanges become more predictable, stronger, and more meaningful. Communication bubbles and partnerships start to be chosen, created, and initiated by the students themselves.

> The parent mentoring group have commented on the impact of Intensive Interaction over many years with their children, noticing their teenage children starting to form close relationships with their peers. They also comment on how their teens now interrupt family members, wanting to play and engage with them, and allow and respond to family members cuddling them. Parents have also noticed them

greeting people more and staying for family gatherings rather than disappearing off to their rooms. To quote one parent mentor:

> *"I have begun to shift my views of my son's autism – whereas I had previously considered him to be often unreachable, suddenly I realised that maybe we were unreachable for him."*

## Challenges and priorities in the Secondary Department

Having established a repertoire of different 'games' with different people, the dynamics have changed for some. Longer periods of time are spent engaging with another person. The interactions may be changed, adapted, and initiated in different ways according to the adult or peer with whom they are communicating (in the same way that we flex the way we speak with our different friends). The activities have become more subtle and complex – but even now it is still not about 'the game'! As the zone of proximal development grows, the practitioner may be able to start to introduce different scenarios by changing the course of the conversation now and again to include things you want to speak about as well. You might even use a bit of sabotage (for example, not having a vital piece of equipment to hand) to promote planning skills and executive function – 'what do I need to do now?'

In the Secondary Department, the curriculum is more formal and less play-focused, but individual needs still dictate priorities for each student and where their focus of learning will be. Students move between specialist rooms for different subjects, and in Key Stage 4 the curriculum focuses upon preparing for exams and gaining qualifications.

For some students, friendships and social interactions with shared interests, hobbies, and occupations really boost their self-worth and well-being. More co-operative working is starting to take place as students have learnt that working in small groups or doing a whole-class activity can be enjoyable (or at least manageable!). Students start learning about perspective taking, risking 'having a go' and making mistakes in a safe, supportive environment with help at hand to unpick if things go wrong.

Staff hold back and let students find the right way as much as possible but need to intervene when emotions fray. Using Intensive Interaction principles of tuning in, pausing, giving time and space, and supporting the individual to co-regulate or self-regulate depending on the situation, individual, and the day are crucial. Because of this, Intensive Interaction has a fundamental role to play within PSHE as well as the communication curriculum, especially for 'in the moment' teaching. Puberty and hormonal changes will always make self-regulation more complicated and difficult during these years and will frequently impact on the individual's ability to manage. Staying with the person through these difficult episodes and letting them know you are still there for them, while keeping you both safe, is hugely important.

It took a great deal of mentoring for me to convey the importance of Intensive Interaction for promoting 'social communication' across secondary, and some staff still sometimes struggle with this idea, seeing behaviour as difficult or stroppy rather than arising from anxiety or miscommunication. To overcome these misconceptions, I held staff meetings for all teaching assistants throughout primary and secondary every four weeks to trouble shoot and share good practice around behaviour management and emotional regulation. Through these meetings, they began to understand how social communication difficulties affected all our students regardless of their cognitive ability. Staff also began to see the essential links between social communication and emotional well-being. Several took the FoCs home to encourage their own families to talk together, and some even changed their seating around so that their focus was on each other rather than the TV.

## What does Intensive Interaction look like in Post-16?

The students (now young adults) will be participating in work experience and part-time college courses. Anxiety may still lead to arousal issues, and this may now manifest as more sexualised behaviour. This is discussed further in Chapter 11, but our approach is to give time to use emotional regulation strategies learnt over years of Intensive Interaction practice and keep working together with parents and carers to ensure our approaches are consistent.

One of the most important communication opportunities for students in Post-16 is the chance to volunteer for early years' playtime supervision. This enables them to work on their interaction skills with the early years students while being supported and mentored by a team of staff, having 20–30-minute slots for play, fun, and learning, while all experiencing the FoCs together. Following this experience, one student volunteered to help at the holiday play scheme and wanted to be mentored to learn how he could improve his communication with others. He worked really hard on this and is now in his second year at college and no longer a volunteer but a paid member of the play scheme staff. By this stage, many of our students have become skilled communicators through years of Intensive Interaction practice, and I must say it is incredibly rewarding to watch a group of students initiating and taking turns when playing a game, completing it successfully without any unwanted behaviour, having fun, and dare I say even cheating!

> Our Post-16 students truly demonstrate the benefit of our whole-school approach to Intensive Interaction and are truly the icing on the cake. It is amazing to see students who joined the school with severe difficulties with emotional regulation, communication, and social communication who have learnt to:
>
> - Work together and co-operate on a task.
> - Share ideas and thoughts.

- 'Chit-chat' about their likes and dislikes.
- Form loving relationships with their families.
- Form friendships with their peers.
- See the value in being with others and sharing interests.
- Increase their sense of self-worth and well-being by knowing that others enjoy their company.

### Challenges and priorities in Post-16

This is not to say that anything comes easy, and social communication can be exhausting for our young people as it takes such a lot of hard work. However, the difference it makes is huge. Prioritising the learning of the FoCs is crucial for these guys as they struggle without them, regardless of cognitive ability. Intensive Interaction helps our young people with autism to understand a world that can seem scary and unpredictable. It equips them with skills to cope, ask questions, share ideas, and sometimes even enjoy communicating with others as they move out from education and into this big, wide, wonderful social world!

## Concluding remarks

So that is the story of my Intensive Interaction journey and the amazing impact it can have when implemented throughout a school. Despite the simplicity of the Intensive Interaction approach, (it only needs you, and maybe a camcorder), despite the lack of SMART targets and objectives, despite the different type of structure, or in fact because of all those things, it is a continual delight to see the amount of learning that it makes possible and to be part of the wonderful things that happen in the process. Intensive Interaction keeps on giving, day by day.

And what about my course project person, Matthew? Well, although it has been many years since I worked closely with him, we still have a very special relationship when we see each other and always greet each other in a 'both tuned together' way. This is the same for all the children and young people with whom I have worked over the years! As Matthew grew older, he became highly studious and exceptionally motivated to achieve things academically. But when this talkative, highly academic young man took a break from Intensive Interaction, his well-being took a dip. Some anxiety-related behaviours that hadn't been seen for a while began to re-emerge, and he seemed a bit lost and unhappy. When the opportunity arose for him to re-engage in Intensive Interaction, this all turned around. His well-being improved, and he regained his spark! This re-confirmed for me and for all our staff that although verbally he can talk for England and is a highly intelligent student, the real key for his progress on every level – cognitive, social, and emotional – is the continued and continuing input of Intensive Interaction.

Thus, for many of the students in my school – indeed for many people with communication and social communication difficulties – there may never be a 'before and after Intensive Interaction'. A 'before and with Intensive Interaction' may, however, be the key to ensuring they are socially included in society and keep on blossoming as human beings.

## References

Hewett, D. (2012). 'What is Intensive Interaction? Curriculum, process and approach'. In: D. Hewett, ed., *Intensive Interaction Theoretical Perspectives*. London: Sage Publications, pp. 137–154.

Mourière, A. (2018). 'Autism and Intensive Interaction, and Intensive Interaction with more able people'. In: D. Hewett, ed., *The Intensive Interaction Handbook*, 2nd ed. London: Sage Publications, pp. 123–129.

# 7. Intensive Interaction within the general communication curriculum

*Lana Bond and Inga K. Serafin*

## Introduction

This chapter will specifically look at how Intensive Interaction sits within the communication curriculum and alongside other communication approaches. Our work exploring how Intensive Interaction fits within the general communication curriculum began when we started working together in our school two years ago. We found we had common philosophies about ways in which to engage with our students and spent many hours talking about how our students developed their communication and what things we found that supported them. We realised that before our students even began to communicate using the various systems on offer, they had to learn all the underlying complex aspects of communication and social communication, such as being with another person, recognising self and other, and creating that social bridge between communicative partners. These Fundamentals of Communication (FoCs) are developed through Intensive Interaction, and this became our common passion (for further information on the FoCs, see Chapter 3).

We come from very different backgrounds. My background (Lana) is in special education, with a main focus of supporting children with complex needs. In 2009 I started the Intensive Interaction coordinator course and the following year completed my master's research on the impact of Intensive Interaction communication learning and the effects on an individual's feelings of well-being. These two combined learning experiences enabled me to study in depth, through observation, recording, and reviewing, the micro details of progress the students made and the impact this had at school and in their wider world. I found it particularly interesting that the emphasis was not on what the learner should be doing, but rather how the more experienced communicator (the teaching staff member) should be supporting this communication and helping to promote the optimum learning environment.

Inga first studied special educational needs in Poland, specialising in education for deaf children, before moving to Australia, where she completed her teacher training. Inga has worked with special needs children for 28 years and throughout her career has used the principles of Intensive Interaction as a route-map for communication and interaction learning with the children with whom she works.

DOI: 10.4324/9781003170839-7

We have both worked and continue to work with people who use Augmented and Alternative Communication (AAC) of various descriptions. When exploring communication development, it is important to recognise and explore all the potential methods and modes that a person might use during their education, or indeed during their lives, for example, eye gaze or iPad programs, or Pragmatic Organisation Dynamic Display (PODD). It is also essential to appreciate that, regardless of the AAC that may be put in place, Intensive Interaction forms the foundation of all communication and social communication. Through learning the FoCs, the gateway is opened to all communication.

Intensive Interaction enables the development of an in-depth relationship with the individual and the ability to tune in with a deep understanding and knowledge of them and their whole being. This knowledge of an individual will help you to pick up on emerging signs of understanding and help them to know that you recognise these signs and understand! These indications might be very subtle – the way they look at you, how they squint one eye or move an eyebrow. By noticing, tuning into, and joining in with these moments following Intensive Interaction principles they will develop them into something more and then use them to intentionally communicate, for example, if they want to continue being with you or need a break. Recognising these changes and developments in exchanges of activities, behaviours, and vocalisations enables us to start understanding the messages that we are being given and thus develop meaningful relationships with our students.

# Developing relationships: the foundation to communication learning

Communication learning is crucial for students with learning difficulties, and all interactions and learning arise from this understanding. The aims of Intensive Interaction are to support the exploration, practice, and rehearsal of the FoCs (Nind and Hewett, 2001). Intensive Interaction, therefore, not only supports the learning of communication skills but also the development of social connections and well-being.

Intensive Interaction builds on Ephraim's original work on 'augmented mothering' (Ephraim, 1986) whereby he proposed using naturalistic interaction based on infant–caregiver interactions with people with severe learning difficulties. During the typical process of child development, caregivers provide infants with lively and social learning environments (Tilstone and Layton, 2004). The natural social and communication process involves the caregiver tuning in and responding to the infant's sounds, gestures, and facial expressions, and through that process the infant learns how to communicate. Intensive Interaction is based on replicating this naturalistic process (Kellet, 2004) which supports the chaotic way in which communication is learned. Within parent-infant interaction, the parent does not pick targets for the infant. Instead, a playful and responsive environment is established by the parent, and the infant initially will be drawn to the smiling face (Schore, 1994). The infant's sympathetic nervous system becomes stimulated, and they experience pleasurable arousal. This can trigger an increased heart rate, and these processes trigger a further biochemical response, leading the infant to feel positive and happy (Panksepp, 1998).

Mutual pleasure is an important aspect of Intensive Interaction because it is this that fuels the motivation to be involved (Nind and Hewett, 1994). These pleasurable experiences positively reinforce the FoCs, making learning more accessible and fun (Gerhardt, 2010). This is partly due to the intrinsic value of the experience which motivates both participants to 'interest and delight one another' (Stern et al., 1977).

## Why we communicate – the different functions of communication

The mutual pleasure comes in part from the engagement in phatic communication or small talk. Through our everyday interactions we use communication to serve different functions. Formal communication or communication with concrete aims or outcomes (CCAO – Hewett et al., 2019) helps to establish details or give instructions. These are important but do not serve an emotional purpose or reflect communication in its entirety. Through the definitions of phatic communion (Malinowski, 1922) and phatic communication (Hewett, 2012), the importance of social connections and a shared moment of togetherness is prioritised over the actual content of a conversation. It can be a simple 'hello, how are you?', where the importance is to make a connection and let someone know you are there, not to receive an accurate health update (Hewett, 2012). It could be a highly animated conversation about something that makes you giggle or a chat over the telephone with your best friend to talk about difficulties at work. These moments can detract from the seriousness of the day and never-ending list of demands that must be fulfilled, as well as enable us to express feelings and emotions.

Maslow's theory of motivation (1970) describes a hierarchy of five levels of basic human need. He states that a person does not feel the second need until the demands of the first have been satisfied, nor the third until the second has been satisfied, and so on. These basic needs are physiological needs; safety needs; the need for love, affection, belonging and esteem; and at the top of the hierarchy, the need for self-actualisation. Maslow's work identifies the importance of a person's well-being; that their feelings of belonging and happiness take priority, before they are in a position to search for self-actualisation and learning. Intensive Interaction is a way of supporting self-expression and understanding while simultaneously developing the FoCs because it allows the learner to control the conversation and attempt to address the issues of their importance. This theory further suggests that meeting the needs of connection and social communication gives the learner opportunities to rehearse the FoCs and gradually equip them to expand their knowledge and further develop their communication.

## Social communication: the engine to all learning

Phatic communication is the learner's opportunity to engage meaningfully with a tuned-in person, to be heard and felt. When we are content and happy, we are more interested in what is happening in the environment, and we seek connections with people. To sustain this state of alertness and positive emotions we need happy hormones. Positive emotions enable the learner to relax into the process of learning. Our role is to create this no pressure/no demand atmosphere and an environment that promotes curiosity. This can be achieved by tuning in and responding to the learner's current behaviour.

Developing relationships that are strong, based on trust, understanding, and mutual pleasure, will later lead to participating in more formal learning.

Learning to communicate occurs in a complex social environment – and thus should not be limited to being examined or perceived as something that happens on an individual level. Instead, it is necessary to think of learning as a social activity involving people, the things they use, the words they speak, the cultural context they are in, and the actions they take (Rogoff, 1998). Knowledge is built within the activity (Scardamalia and Bereiter, 2006).

Intensive Interaction is a way of being that removes barriers and promotes the naturalistic communication learning process whilst simultaneously offering genuine connections. By creating these moments where the student is in control of content and flow, this leads to the learner feeling free to express themselves in whichever way they choose, about whatever they choose. Referring back to Maslow's hierarchy of motivation these expressions could be relating to a personal need such as hunger, being uncomfortable, or the need for a social connection and chit-chat.

Learners at early levels of development are generally at a pre-symbolic or emergent stage of cognitive or communication development and may therefore be unable to understand signs and symbols. Their communication may be pre-verbal, possibly including eye gaze, gesture, movement, and vocalisation, which will form the core of their early interactions around the FoCs. However, continued frequent rehearsal of the FoCs may, over time, lead to a point of understanding at which students are more receptive to learning signs, symbols, and speech. It is important to recognise that as humans are social creatures, the need for social connection and communication is present throughout life regardless of age or ability. The learning of language or being a competent user of AAC devices does not remove that social need. Social communication is the foundation upon which all other communication learning builds. Therefore, even if a child can speak or use AAC, the curriculum must still address and prioritise social communication. The learners' right to social communication should be present throughout and in all aspects of their lives and should therefore be reflected as central to the communication curriculum.

As in typical development, phatic or purely social interactions allow the learner to practice and rehearse the FoCs. As the learner gains a deeper understanding of the FoCs they are more able to express their wants and needs. Separating phatic communication from CCAOs can negatively affect communication learning. It is through the process of total communication exploration that the learner can try to make sense of communication and understand why communicating with another person can be good. The practitioner must recognise these moments when they occur to facilitate learning in either or both of these categories.

# Case study: Ruby

This example illustrates the learning journey for Ruby, a young lady with PMLD and limited mobility. During focused Intensive Interaction sessions, I observed that Ruby would use eye gaze to seemingly look at items. Ruby would fix her gaze and only return to look at me once I had acknowledged what she was looking at by commenting on it. Over time, the consistency of my responses to Ruby's eye gaze developed in a back-and-forth conversation in which she would gaze at something and wait for a response from me. I explored different responses, such as asking easy yes and no questions or using a simple verbal commentary. 'Are you looking at the door?' or 'Do you know that's a camera?' – as she grinned towards the lens.

How this example relates to the communication curriculum:

- By rehearsing the FoCs within pleasurable and meaningful activities, Ruby was able to consolidate the fundamental skills required to be able to understand yes/no questions.
- This developed into Ruby being able to use her gaze to subsequently express her wants and needs.
- Intensive Interaction input throughout the day as well as regular Intensive Interaction sessions enabled Ruby to explore communication and for the team to observe the communication skills she already possessed.
- By the time Ruby left secondary school, she had a handbag on her wheelchair containing all her favourite and personal items that she could request and discuss (albeit without words) at her will. A photo of the bag on the arm of her chair would enable her to either request the bag or initiate a 'conversation'.
- By prioritising the social aspect of communication and the learning of the FoCs, Ruby gradually learnt to use a variety of ways to communicate in different situations to serve different functions:
    o Visual support using photos.
    o Using eye gaze.
    o Using eye pointing.
    o Using facial expressions.
    o Using vocalisation.

---

The learning of the FoCs is not a tick-box exercise, by which one day one learns to give eye contact and the next can concentrate on turn-taking. Reflecting on the minute changes in the learner's communication abilities helps build up detailed information of exactly how the learner is communicating, what they are motivated to do or communicate about, and where they are in terms of communication development and understanding the FoCs. With this information it is possible to plan separate skill-based sessions to build upon their current understanding. Ruby would participate in separate eye-gaze sessions where the specific objectives were set prior to the session. Throughout the sessions members of staff would utilise the principles of Intensive Interaction to support the flow and help to create moments of excitement and interest. Phatic communication was woven into these sessions even though more focused on CCAOs to replicate natural communication where the two are hand in hand and not separate from each other.

## Case study: Annie

Annie has global developmental delay, she wears glasses, she can slide/move her arms across her tray, she can move her fingers, and she is pre-verbal. When I started working with Annie she was disengaged during adult-led activities and would often turn her face away, close her eyes, or hang her head down.

Through Intensive Interaction, we learnt to tune in to the pattern of Annie's vocalisations and emotional responses and gradually build tolerance, trust, and finding a topic of conversation. Hearing the staff using her vocal sounds with exaggeration intrigued Annie enough to look for the source of the sound (the practitioner), and she would sustain her gaze and smile or move her hands on the tray.

Over time Annie started smiling when her favourite adult was approaching in anticipation of a joyful interaction. Pausing and waiting, to give her time to respond and reinitiate, encouraged her to be more involved in the interactions and led to Annie setting the rules, timing, and taking the lead. She learnt how to combine vocalisations and eye pointing, and she was showing great disappointment when the adult didn't understand her. Annie's focus has changed from just observing and responding. She has begun:

- Initiating interactions.
- Anticipating social interaction.
- Sustaining social interaction.
- Decreasing in withdrawal from others.
- Showing greater tolerance.
- Observing others.
- Participating spontaneously.

In later stages this led to using specific objects and objects of reference to give her another tool to express herself.

> # Case study: Andy
>
> Andy has a diagnosis of autism, global developmental delay, and has difficulty with depth perception and peripheral vision. When he arrived in our class, he communicated his needs and wants by using gestures and frustrated vocalisations but avoided other contact with people; therefore any adult led activity would end up in a fiasco. Andy's favourite place was on the edge of the mat, becoming absorbed in lining up and making patterns from similar shaped objects (e.g. markers); he could repeat this activity indefinitely. When we introduced Intensive Interaction with him, Andy allowed the adult to play near him using their own set of objects but moved his markers to the other side, thus taking control.
>
> Together we developed this game further into sharing resources, swapping items, taking turns, and adding happy vocalisations. Andy began to look up and to meet the adult's eyes willingly for the first time. He has begun changing focus from the objects to the adult and waiting for an invitation to play a vocal game.
>
> The development of the FoCs and social communication took priority over his repetitive play, and Andy began to:
>
> - Share space with another person.
> - Enjoy the interactions and attend to the person whom he was with.
> - Sustain his eye gaze during interactions.
> - Use a range of facial expressions and gestures (smiling and pointing).
> - Effectively use shared attention to request and bring attention to what he was doing.
>
> Consistently responding to his communicative behaviours led to Andy using a variety of other ways of communicating, including natural gestures, photos, some symbols, and switches for requesting. His communication system has developed over time facilitated by close observation and scaffolding support from the adults.

## Intensive Interaction across the communication curriculum

There is a distinct difference between following a structured communication approach using AAC (including signs and photos) and Intensive Interaction. Approaches that are 'skill orientated' are frequently strictly structured. They often omit social exchanges, or the social exchanges are highly artificial and therefore restrict and devalue their psychological/emotional importance. It is possible, however, to use elements in combination to provide a range of strategies for pupils to use when communicating. For example, by using sustained gaze and vocal sounds to get attention, using eye pointing to indicate need and then confirming the choice with a smile or a nod.

> Humans are social beings, and we must recognise the social aspect of communication. As practitioners and professionals, we must ensure that our focus is not entirely on CCAOs, learning to express wants and needs through a predesigned system. If the learner does not have a good understanding of the FoCs they will always need external support, such as prompts and cues. This social aspect of communication is crucial when providing our pupils with the range of strategies to initiate, sustain, and maintain shared attention. It will equip the young person with the set of skills and emotional intelligence for the future journey in our complex and increasingly demanding world.

For the ultimate success of a communication curriculum, it must be central to other school documents to cement communication as an ethos, not a standalone policy. The principles of Intensive Interaction can be used across the curriculum throughout the school day as a way of being with the students. This practice will impact upon wider school policy, such as the behaviour policy. It is now universally acknowledged that all behaviour is communication (Imray and Hewett, 2015), and approaches which serve to connect with and understand the learner are now more commonly written in behaviour support plans. Intensive Interaction is seen as a way of reducing demand and fostering a positive connection that can support de-escalation, thereby re-establishing a positive learning and social environment or relationship. (For more on how Intensive Interaction impacts policy, see Chapter 12).

There are a variety of different teaching approaches aimed at supporting the learning of communication skills in schools. Through the previous examples it is possible to see that Intensive Interaction can be used alongside other elements of communication systems to enable the learner to communicate in a way in which they can access themselves and be extended by the use of symbols, pictures, signs, AAC, etc.

> There is a danger in schools of relying too heavily on goal-directed functional communication, that is, communication that serves a concrete purpose, to impart or gain information. Some teaching approaches focus purely on functional communication, and this does not enable a means of building 'sustained and sociable two-way communication' (Firth, Berry and Irvine, 2010, p. 77).

## Concluding remarks

The process of Intensive Interaction allows time to be given to observing and understanding a student's natural communication skills and interests. Building upon this in a meaningful way and removing barriers to the learner's inclusion allows them to express themselves to meet their social and emotional needs.

The FoCs are essential and foundational learning in communication and social understanding. They include developing the ability to attend to a person, enjoying spending time together and engaging in joint attention. Through the use of Intensive Interaction, a repertoire of sequences of activities is developed, encouraging learner-led initiations and turn-taking. Each participant uses eye contact, facial expression, physical contact, and vocalisations. Through this interactive process the learner can begin to understand the FoCs, the emotions behind them, and how to read and interpret them in the behaviours of others. The FoCs therefore underpin all learning and in turn must be the foundation of the communication curriculum.

As a team, we value the importance of Intensive Interaction moments as we recognise that progress made in general has its roots in well-rehearsed FoCs. The support of social encounters in a relaxed and responsive atmosphere and having the safety of trusting relationships helps students to be settled during adult-led activities and engage in the process. Thus, with a focus on social communication and social participation subsequent progress with CCAOs can then become evident and occur more naturally and in context.

Intensive Interaction should be embedded as a way of being – as a thread that runs through the school day. It should be reflected in the culture of the school. This is best achieved through good practice, through writing it into multiple school policies, and ensuring that the FoCs are an integral part of the curriculum.

# References

Ephraim, G. (1986). *A Brief Introduction to Augmented Mothering*. Playtrac Pamphlet. Radlett, Herts: Harperbury Hospital School.

Firth, G., Berry, R. and Irvine, C. (2010). *Understanding Intensive Interaction*. London: Jessica Kingsley Publishers.

Gerhardt, S. (2010). *Why Love Matters; How Affection Shapes a Baby's Brain*. New York: Routledge.

Hewett, D. (2012). 'Blind frogs: The nature of human communication and Intensive Interaction'. In: D. Hewett, ed., *Intensive Interaction: Theoretical Perspectives*. London: Sage Publications, pp. 4–21.

Hewett, D., Calveley, J., McKim, J. and Mourière, A. (2019). Communication, human rights and Intensive Interaction. *PMLD Link*, 31(1), Issue 92, pp. 8–10.

Imray, P. and Hewett, D. (2015). 'Challenging behaviour and the curriculum'. In: P. Lacey, R. Ashdown, P. Jones, H. Lawson and M. Pipe, eds., *The Routledge Companion to Severe, Profound and Multiple Learning Difficulties*. London: Routledge.

Kellet, M. (2004). Intensive Interaction in the inclusive classroom: Using interactive pedagogy to connect with students who are hardest to reach. *Westminster Studies in Education*, 27(2), pp. 175–188.

Malinowski, B. (1922). *Argonauts of the Western Pacific: An Account of Native Enterprise and Adventure in the Archipelago of Melanesian New Guinea*. London: Routledge.

Maslow, A. H. (1970). *Motivation and Personality*. New York: Harper and Row.

Nind, M. and Hewett, D. (1994). *Access to Communication: Developing the Basics of Communication with People with Severe Learning Difficulties Through Intensive Interaction*. London: David Fulton.

Nind, M. and Hewett, D. (2001). *A Practical Guide to Intensive Interaction*. Glasgow: BILD.

Panksepp, J. (1998). *Affective Neuroscience: The Foundations of Human and Animal Emotions*. Oxford: Oxford University Press.

Rogoff, B. (1998). 'Cognition, perception and language: Handbook of child psychology'. In: D. Kuhn and R. S. Siegler, eds., *Cognition, Perception and Language*, 5th ed. New York: John Wiley and Sons, pp. 679–744.

Scardamalia, M. and Bereiter, C. (2006). 'Learning in activity'. In: R. K. Sawyer, ed., *The Cambridge Handbook of the Learning Sciences*. Cambridge: Cambridge University Press, pp. 97–118.

Schore, A. (1994). *Affect Regulation and the Origins of the Self*. Hillsdale, NJ: Lawrence Erlbaum Associates Inc.

Stern, D. N., Beebe, B., Jaffe, J. and Bennett, S. L. (1977). 'The infant's stimulus world during social interaction: A study of caregiver behaviors with particular reference to repetition timing'. In: H. R. Schaffer, ed., *Studies in Mother – Infant Interaction*. New York: Academic Press, pp. 177–202.

Tilstone, C. and Layton, L. (2004). *Child Development and Teaching Pupils with Special Educational Needs*. London: Routledge.

# 8. Intensive Interaction within our holistic and child-centred approach at Brøndagerskolen

*Sanne Laudrup and Pernille Hasseriis Noach*

## Brøndagerskolen in Denmark

Brøndagerskolen is a special school for children and young people with autism spectrum disorder (ASD), many of whom have additional learning difficulties. This chapter will describe our ethos and child-centred approach at Brøndagerskolen. It will also explore all the developmental opportunities we are finding through working towards embedding Intensive Interaction in our school's communication, social communication, and broader curriculum.

Our student group is characterised by a broad range of developmental levels, spanning from pupils at early levels of development in all areas to pupils whose general cognitive abilities are not affected. Covering 1st–11th grades, the school currently has 93 students enrolled. The children are divided into 15 groups of approximately 5–7 students each, with one member of staff working with two students at a time. Students are divided primarily by age, so each group includes individuals of various cognitive abilities. There are three students on individual programs who each have their own team of staff.

Brøndagerskolen was established in 1971 as a special school with affiliated teachers and assistants and after-school provision for the students staffed by pedagogues and assistants. In Denmark, more than other countries, it is customary for trained pedagogues to work across a broad spectrum of nurseries, kindergartens, schools, clubs, group homes, care facilities, and in the community, using their expertise to create a holistic learning environment for children, young people, and adults. At our school the pedagogues help to support the students' special needs and prerequisites. They are trained for early-years learning and have competencies to develop students from a lifelong perspective with a focus on well-being and social development.

In 1993, the structure of Brøndagerskolen was reorganised to provide an *integrated scheme*, combining the school and after-school provision into a single program for children and young people with ASD and learning difficulties. Since then, teachers, pedagogues, and assistants have worked side by side, creating a more

DOI: 10.4324/9781003170839-8

cohesive day for each student. Every team features two teachers, two pedagogues, and additional assistants who meet weekly to ensure a consistent, interdisciplinary approach. Separate meetings are also held for each of the three professional groups, plus full staff meetings.

There is a large overlap in the professional abilities of the teachers and pedagogues. Yet, in addition to their common ethos and understanding each group also has a unique set of knowledge which, when combined, provides a more thorough understanding of every child's needs.

From the beginning of the integrated scheme, the school has been defined by its interdisciplinary approach and access to a highly qualified team of professionals. This special team consists of:

- Two pedagogical supervisors.
- Two speech and language therapists.
- One psychologist.
- One physiotherapist.
- One occupational therapist.
- One health nurse.
- One education supervisor.

These special team members use their specific professional areas of expertise to support in three ways: contributing to interdisciplinary assessments of each student's abilities and potential, supporting staff with gaining a more thorough understanding of their students' competences and potential, and advising parents throughout their child's education.

## Brøndagerskolen values

In the process of creating this integrated scheme, the school's values were defined and continue to be defined as follows:

- Give the individual student a high degree of independence and self-worth.
- Prepare the students for an active youth and adult life.
- Give students guidance based on professional expertise and advanced knowledge within teaching and social pedagogy.
- Maintain a dynamic pedagogical practice by constantly developing new methods and pedagogical paths.
- Ensure an interdisciplinary pedagogical environment.
- Organise vocational courses with respect to the individual student's uniqueness, interests, and potential.

# Brøndagerskolen curriculum

In 1999, work began on compiling the school's own curriculum to guarantee that the integrated school/after-school program always offered variety while focusing on nurturing individual students' full potential. Due to the varying degree of ASD amongst the students, it was crucial for the curriculum to meet the needs of the entire group.

Teaching at Brøndagerskolen is much more than merely teaching subjects. Applying the concept of teaching to its fullest, we ensure that our understanding of a child's needs is apparent at all times. Our teaching is guided by the curriculum. This functions as a tool to help staff plan specific goals for individual students. We also work collaboratively with parents to prioritise students' strengths, opportunities, and overall potential for skill development.

The curriculum is the foundation of everything we do at Brøndagerskolen. However, it is not a fixed document. It is evaluated every year by all professionally trained employees to make sure the structure and content remain relevant. This dynamic process has enabled us to refine the curriculum to the following eight areas around which the students' individual learning is built:

- Key subjects (math, Danish, etc.).
- Social.
- Communication.
- Motor skills.
- Self-help.
- Everyday skills.
- Community life.
- Citizenship.
- Leisure time.

> As a part of our school's culture and dynamic process of curriculum development, we continually explore new initiatives that can improve the way we work with the individual children. We have an eclectic approach and want to acquire new knowledge and improve our practice, whilst always reflecting upon how new methods correspond with our understanding of autism and comorbid conditions.

The school offers staff training through conferences and courses, and, with the help of a development group, invites speakers to the school to teach and inspire the staff. In recent years, we have enjoyed the presence of Dr Dave Hewett, who has twice visited the school to provide training, participate in, and give feedback on Intensive

Interaction sessions. These inspirational visits have played an essential role in fostering the school's interest in exploring Intensive Interaction as a highly valuable and pertinent approach for working with the children.

# The five dimensions

The overarching pedagogical principles and methods of our curriculum are encompassed by five dimensions, which stem from humanistic thinking and a set of values around structured teaching. Intensive Interaction principles (Hewett, 2018) are highly aligned with these five dimensions and fit well with our focus upon child-centred learning and knowledge of our students as individuals.

The five dimensions align with the school's values and are not placed in a specific order.

## The individual child

Our focus is always upon the individual child. When children begin at Brøndagerskolen, it is important for us to know as much as possible about them. We study each child's entire medical record, including personal accounts and diagnosis. We meet with professionals from their previous setting and carry out an in-depth induction meeting with parents during which we talk about the child's interests, developmental and medical history. Six months after starting school, we review the child's progress and use our knowledge of their cognitive, communicative, social, emotional, sensory, and motor abilities to create an individualised program. Progress is reviewed annually, and new targets are agreed upon with input from parents and members of the special team.

In eighth grade a further interdisciplinary meeting is held with parents to support the child's move from primary school, identifying their skills, strengths, and overall potential to work. This builds towards finding a suitable program for each student when they graduate from Brøndagerskolen. At every stage, our approach is child-centred, striving to engage them in activities incorporating their interests which are developmentally pertinent and intrinsically motivating.

Because Intensive Interaction focuses at all times on the individual child's needs and is child-led and child-centred, the approach is highly compatible with the way we work at the school.

## Understanding autism

All teachers and pedagogues participate in the school's introductory course to acquire a baseline knowledge of autism, possible comorbidities, and potential barriers to learning. It is critical to understand that autism is a congenital, neurologically pervasive developmental disorder which causes the individual to perceive, understand, and navigate the world in a different manner. Having autism can have a huge effect on interaction and communication with others, which is something we as staff members must be aware of and respect. As individuals with autism must be understood on their own terms, we must respect that they represent a different culture – a culture they have the right to preserve. This means that the individual shall, of course, have the right to preserve his or her interests and uniqueness.

## Our holistic and child-centred approach

We consider that Intensive Interaction is an ideal approach for people with ASD, enabling them to work on all the complex emotional and social difficulties through non-pressurised, relaxed, and playful activities.

### Making sense for the child

As we commonly say in Denmark, 'What makes sense for you, is not necessarily the same that makes sense for me'.

Our students, like all children with autism, benefit from a high degree of visual support. At Brøndagerskolen these are always tailored and customised to create meaning and predictability for each child. For someone with ASD and learning difficulties, it can be a struggle to fully recognise and understand structure and possibilities. So, when we create a specific, meaningful structure for a child, we consider four main aspects of physical organisation, schedule, work systems, and instructions.

In organising the physical surroundings, we create opportunities to develop the individual's potential for independence and expertise by defining areas where different activities will take place. We use individualised visual schedules to support our students to understand what will occur throughout the school day. Our work systems for activities and assignments are also highly visually structured to clarify to each student what will happen, for how long it will happen, and what will happen afterwards.

> If we can make our communication more understandable, we can increase the potential for the individual to communicate, as well as increase the likelihood of greater well-being. When we work with children and young people with severe communication and learning disabilities, we have a special responsibility to meet the child at their level. This means continuously searching for and adapting to what makes the most sense for the child.

It is essential to make sure that the structure does not become rigid and constraining. It must be dynamic, humanistic, flexible, and individually designed to provide a meaningful structure that the child can understand and feel comfortable within. By seeking the correct approach, we can develop unique strategies that make sense for each child.

When the child's world becomes understandable and they feel safe, we know we have created the optimal setting where great Intensive Interaction can take place.

### Lifelong perspective

The school's program covers a period of 11 years. This is an important, yet also very short, period in a person's life. That said, autism is a lifelong disability, meaning it is important that we think with a lifelong perspective. One of the most important things for us to understand is that our job is to give our students strategies and options for action that will allow them to do as well as possible in the future.

The value of a lifelong perspective is also of great importance in Intensive Interaction. It is essential to see our little ones at six as the adult they will become and the skills they need to get them there.

## Dynamic practice

> 'If assessment for learning is at the heart of the process then the pupil is at the centre, not the curriculum' (Lacey, 2010, p. 18).

As our school advocates dynamic practice, we use continuous assessment with our students. Our student group with ASD often has a very spiky developmental profile, and it can therefore be especially difficult to know where the nearest developmental zone lies. Furthermore, the student may have acquired very specific knowledge about their special interests. Therefore, an evaluation of the nearest developmental zone is an important tool in our teaching so we can then set relevant, individually tailored, and meaningful teaching goals.

Our whole philosophy of constantly searching for approaches that support our children with their communication, social communication, and social understanding is what led us to Intensive Interaction. This same philosophy is now inspiring us to integrate and embed Intensive Interaction into our daily practice.

# Intensive Interaction at the school

After Hewett's inspirational visit, we wanted to build upon the enthusiasm that had been generated about Intensive Interaction. The management decided to train us as Intensive Interaction Coordinators and formed an Intensive Interaction committee, of which we became a part.

Between Hewett's two visits, we held presentations for the three different professional groups, where we reviewed the Fundamentals of Communication (FoCs), as well as the principles behind Intensive Interaction. We discussed our experience with establishing Intensive Interaction sessions with individual students in our own teams and showed videos about it.

A folder about Intensive Interaction, to which all the staff have access, was created on our internal server. This includes information about the FoCs, principles, progress tracks, and recording sheets. Additionally, there are uploaded videos of diverse Intensive Interaction sessions with children from the school, as well as Hewett's feedback to the staff from the same sessions.

Through our training as Intensive Interaction Coordinators, we have mentored two colleagues. We chose a mentee in each of our teams because we wanted to work closely together during the process. We wanted to

Our holistic and child-centred approach

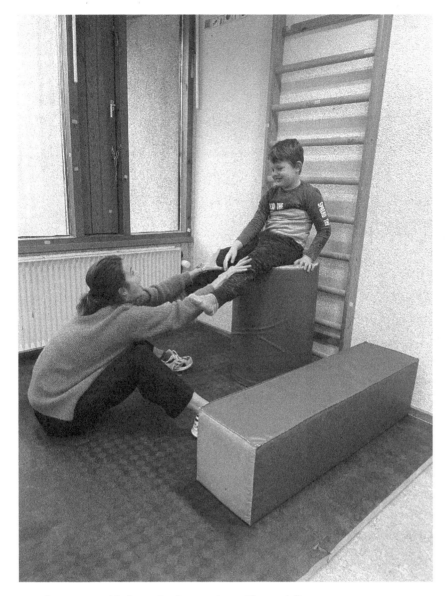

**Figure 8.1** Photo – student engaged in Intensive Interaction with an adult

create room for mutual observations, reflections, and inspiration for our Intensive Interaction sessions. It gave our mentees opportunities to get comfortable with the techniques and principles of Intensive Interaction in a safe and supportive environment. It has been an instructive and fruitful process that has created more awareness of Intensive Interaction within our entire teams.

> As Coordinators we need to keep developing our own Intensive Interaction practices and with the mentoring process, we have had great opportunities to do so. We have held reflection groups for interested members of staff to share experiences and discuss any queries or issues that have arisen. We have been looking at a lot of videos, had discussions, and reflected upon them to continue the embedding of Intensive Interaction within the school. We need each other's support to maintain best practice.

Given that we are a school, there are some obvious goals that we must fulfil. Intensive Interaction is a process-central approach (see Chapter 4), and it has therefore been important for us to make clear that it is a serious and well-founded piece of work being carried out, even though it does not set measurable goals. Therefore, we have described the purpose, approach, and development in our annual plans. Furthermore, at our meetings with parents and authorities, we have documented our work by sharing recorded progress and videos of the individual child.

# Intensive Interaction in the classroom

## Individual needs

We have described earlier how Brøndagerskolen is a school with a long tradition of seeing the entirety of an individual – including all needs, opportunities, and challenges. It is also essential to meet the child as an individual when it comes to Intensive Interaction. We must be curious about who the child is. What makes the child happy? Where does the child feel secure?

Our students are just as unique as the rest of us. For example, just as one child can find it calming and peaceful to stand beneath trees on the playground, it can be stressful and overstimulating for another child to notice wind on their face, a change in temperature, and/or the sounds around them.

Many children with ASD need predictable and specific preparation. They can face challenges with, for example, stress and high arousal. It is therefore important that we observe and take all elements of the child into account when we organise Intensive Interaction at our school. We must not mistakenly assume that we can create a single Intensive Interaction setting that makes sense for all children, but rather we must seek to create opportunities for Intensive Interaction in many contexts.

## Learning environments

When we moved into the school's premises, it was arranged in a normal, open classroom setup. Today, our classrooms are designed differently. Smaller spaces are built in the classrooms to accommodate many different needs. In some learning situations, we need floor space and open places, while in others we need to partition individual students between different activities. Our classrooms must help the child to feel secure and maintain focus, but at the same time we must be attentive to stimulating motor and sensory abilities. With shelves, tables, and partitions all on wheels, we can easily reorganise everything based on what we need at a given time. In addition to being on wheels, our staff chairs are also adjustable, allowing us to move down to eye level with the child and providing opportunities for optimal positioning for Intensive Interaction.

We have hooks in the ceiling to attach various swings, rope ladders, and hammocks, depending on which activities we have planned and the student's wants or needs. We also have beanbags and mattresses that can be folded or moved if the student wishes to play or relax. Our learning environments are characterised by general knowledge of early-years development and sensory modulation.

Our experience shows that these learning environments are ideal for establishing quality Intensive Interaction moments. When a child is, for example, on a swing, we can limit the area with a partition and lay a few mattresses on the ground beneath the swing. This allows the adult to sit or lay down comfortably and, at the same time, creates the opportunity for the child to feel comfortable in close interaction with the adult.

The hallway area outside the classrooms is used in many ways at our school. An individual child can stimulate motor or sensory abilities by riding a scooter or roller skating in the hall, while also having the opportunity to interact with children from other classes. Benches are placed in various locations around the halls, and in one area, space has been created to hang out alone or with another in a little hiding place. As staff, the hallway area offers opportunities for Intensive Interaction sessions with the children.

Our outdoor environment includes tables, benches, swings, sandboxes, seesaws, and trampolines, all of which have proven helpful in creating a good setting for Intensive Interaction.

## Balance of the day

Providing the child with understanding and predictability is essential to create a daily balance. It is therefore important for us to customise a structure that gives the child the necessary information and is fully understandable to them.

When we plan the child's day, we must consider balance and well-being. We seek to create a balance between learning activities, activities of a more motor and sensory nature, as well as different break time activities. Again, the needs of the child determine when a break is warranted. Is there a need for exercise, play, calm, or relaxation? When we create break areas that accommodate the child's needs, we increase the potential for well-being and balance.

Staff typically work together with two or three children at a time. This demands special focus and organisation to create the one-to-one time that is necessary for Intensive Interaction. One-to-one time creates an opportunity for staff to take time to tune in and be available to follow the child's lead. They can be more relaxed and present in the moment knowing that other staff are taking responsibility for the rest of the class. This feeling usually spreads to the child, which together with the environment, creates great opportunities for beautiful Intensive Interaction sessions.

When we plan time for Intensive Interaction, we must still remember to consider the child's needs. This means finding out whether the child, for example, needs to know who he or she will be together with, where an activity will take place, or how long an activity will last. This may seem to challenge some of the thoughts behind Intensive Interaction, such as the natural and playful approach, but the child's own terms must not be forgotten. When we remember to apply our knowledge of each individual, we see development in the children of Brøndagerskolen. Maybe it is an extra, reassuring detail of a timer, or maybe it is a picture of a specific adult in the play area that gives the child the familiarity he or she needs.

> Intensive Interaction, of course, does not only take place during planned time periods, as it is an approach that can happen spontaneously in any environment. It can take place in the coat room or bathroom, during gymnastics or learning activities. In short, Intensive Interaction can occur anywhere.

We understand that we do not always have time in class, and that other places may not be appropriate (e.g. walking near traffic). Yet, while we recognise we may not always have time for longer Intensive Interaction sessions, we make sure to always acknowledge and follow the child's lead. Intensive Interaction has become a part of the daily communication in our two classes.

## Teamwork

Working across several disciplines and with various sets of specialised eyes on the children, opinions sometimes diverge regarding what should be prioritised in our teaching. We are therefore forced to find a balance and compromise on what is most important to spend teaching time on. We have had professional discussions within the teams about how to prioritise our one-to-one time with the children. Rather than class teaching, our teaching within all competence areas is most often one-to-one. As school staff, teachers have a duty to teach the key subjects, but we must be aware that when we choose a subject to teach, we are also choosing not to teach other subjects. We make the same considerations when we decide to implement Intensive Interaction in our teams. We have had, however, good experiences with integrating Intensive Interaction with everything we had previously done at the school – making it not either/or, but a both/and.

Our experience with getting the full extent of Intensive Interaction out in the teams has been the result of modelling best practice. We have been conscious about making Intensive Interaction visible in many different settings and with many different children. We have used time during our team meetings to explain what Intensive Interaction is and why we do what we do. We have explained the FoCs and, with the help of videos, illustrated the principles that we use.

In our teams we have discussed the technical aspects of getting quality film recordings and involved our team members in helping to film both spontaneous and planned Intensive Interaction sessions. We have discussed the willingness to be flexible in the everyday. It has been a strength of our team members to have been, on occasion, adaptable and helpful, taking over working with other children if there was suddenly a child who wanted to initiate Intensive Interaction.

Gradually, as children in our teams have become more accustomed to the Intensive Interaction approach, it has been easier for us to join them for short periods of time and then acknowledge that we can continue with Intensive Interaction later. While it is our reality that we cannot always respond to all cues and initiatives from all children, it is important that we make the effort to ensure that all children feel acknowledged, even if only for a brief moment.

In our teams we have discussed our own insecurities, as well as the considerations and challenges with which we have dealt to demystify everything and remove any potential expectations or pressure. We have made the effort to explain that we each have different personal boundaries and that it is important that those in the team respect these differences.

> Our teams have collectively increased the focus on the development of individual students within Intensive Interaction. We have used progress tracks, which hang in the classrooms along with a pencil, to make it easy to take the necessary notes. We have been clear that everyone on the team, regardless of role or education, is equally responsible for writing their observations down. This means that we as a team have established a common language, allowing us to rejoice and be excited together about the development of the students.

# Considerations in embedding Intensive Interaction

Intensive Interaction is still new at Brøndagerskolen, but we are looking forward to the coming years of embedding the approach throughout the school and creating a responsive environment. We have become Intensive Interaction Coordinators and have a lot of ideas and thoughts about how we can incorporate these further into our school. We have chosen to highlight six of these areas.

## Staff training

When we further implement Intensive Interaction within the school, it will be necessary that all staff have knowledge of the approach. There is an obvious opportunity for us as Coordinators, to include Intensive Interaction as a permanent part of the school's induction course for new members of staff. This way we can ensure that all future staff have knowledge of Intensive Interaction, as well as awareness of us as the school's Coordinators. Moreover, we would also like to offer mentoring courses for individual members of staff.

We wish to offer Intensive Interaction workshops for all staff. It is important that there is an opportunity for them to be inspired together with other colleagues across all teams. Some example subjects could be:

- How to start?
- Video as documentation and a working tool.

- Personal boundaries.
- How do we prioritize the 1:1 time?

### The teams
We wish to participate in team group meetings, where we can offer advice and inspiration. We will qualify the conversations by including the FoCs 1 and 2 (see Chapter 3), progress recording, assessment of the child's behaviour, and the principles of Intensive Interaction. We will also be able to provide advice on 'tuning in' to specific children.

### The specialists
We believe that a collaboration between the school's specialists will be fruitful. We will be able to offer observations and Intensive Interaction sessions with a selected child. We will also be able to provide feedback to the child's team and talk with the specialist.

### The parents
It is important that we also involve the parents and provide them with knowledge of Intensive Interaction. We wish to describe Intensive Interaction in a community parent meeting. Another area of focus could be supporting staff in conveying Intensive Interaction to the parents.

### The management
The management team is a crucial ally in our work to embed the approach. They create the framework when we, together, must find the way to anchor Intensive Interaction in Brøndagerskolen.

### The curriculum
The school's curriculum is a dynamic, continuously modified work tool. There are already plans about how Intensive Interaction will be included, and we must discuss how Intensive Interaction can be implemented in the curriculum. For example, how do we make space for goals of communication and early social interaction that are not immediately measurable but no less essential to include and relate to? Could we include FoCs 1 and 2 in the curriculum? Could videos, progress tracks, and recording sheets be used to measure development? Would it be beneficial to integrate the social and the communication aspects for early-years learners?

## Concluding remarks

We have made great progress since Dave Hewett's first visits to Brøndagerskolen, and it has been exciting to see how the principles and philosophy of Intensive Interaction are so closely aligned with our school's values. The dissemination of this approach is continuing as we build on staff's enthusiasm and our own knowledge as Intensive Interaction Coordinators. It will be exciting work that we look forward to developing.

## References

Hewett, D. (ed.) (2018). *The Intensive Interaction Handbook*. 2nd ed. London: Sage Publications.

Lacey, P. (2010). Smart and scruffy targets. *SLD Experience*, 57, pp. 16–21.

# 9. Developing the Fundamentals of Communication through free-flow play

*Julie Cassidy and Katy Snell*

## Background

In this chapter we will describe how, after completing a postgraduate course, Froebel Certificate in Early Childhood at Roehampton University, we developed a free-flow play project with two groups of reception-age children with autism and additional severe learning difficulties. 'In free-flow play children move freely, usually indoors and outdoors making choices as they go, about what they want to play with and with whom' (Yates, 2018, p. 354).

Before getting into the main part of this chapter we need to discuss how this project came about. We hope our experience may be of support to practitioners looking to change the ethos and delivery of play and prioritise the Fundamentals of Communication (FoCs) learning within your place of work.

We are both teachers of children with profound and multiple learning difficulties (PMLD) and complex needs, severe learning difficulties (SLD), and children with autism and additional learning difficulties. Like Dave Hewett (see Chapter 2), we both started our journey into special education in the 1980s, teaching and volunteering with 'hard to reach' young people in hospital schools.

Between us we have notched up over 50 years of teaching experience. During this time, we have seen teaching methods and approaches in special education come and go, and some have even reappeared in a new form and with a new name.

We are both interactionists, committed to developing social communication and the FoCs by following a child's lead, developing emotional regulation, and building relationships with them. We have both been advocates of Intensive Interaction for more than 30 years after reading *Access to Communication* (Nind and Hewett, 1994) back in the 1990s.

In stark contrast, we were both trained in behaviour modification and its offshoot, task analysis, as part of our teacher training. This approach is based on the work of psychologist B.F. Skinner (see Chapter 2). In his

DOI: 10.4324/9781003170839-9

view, learning is a behaviour determined by its consequences and reinforcements, which make the behaviour more (or less) likely to happen again.

In recent years behaviourism has made a 'come back' in the form of applied behaviour analysis and the discrete trial teaching approach, which focuses upon adult-directed tasks, skills-based activities with an emphasis on compliance training, verbal and physical prompts, and reinforcing the targeted behaviour to shape it (Anderson, 2007).

A few years ago this approach played a significant role in the teaching and learning process in the autism department of our school. In contrast, in our SLD/PMLD department play-based approaches played a more significant role as Intensive Interaction was naturally woven into the fabric of the daily curriculum.

Over time, the vision and ethos of our school began to change, and the two departments merged closer together in their approaches. This began to evolve when the principles of the Early Years Foundation Stage (Department for Education, 2017) were adopted throughout the school with play, intrinsic motivation, engagement, and enabling environments at its core.

As this was developing, Julie, together with the deputy head and Early Years leader, began to research, develop, and write our own bespoke, the 'Mandeville Developmental Curriculum and Assessment Tool'. This focused on the development and assessment of early communication and cognitive skills through play-based approaches.

> 'In play a child always behaves beyond his (average age) ability, above his daily behaviour; in play it is as though he were a head taller than himself. As in the focus of a magnifying glass, play contains all the developmental tendencies in a condensed form and is itself a major source of development'.
> (Vygotsky, 1978, p. 102)

The interactionist approach had begun to take root across the school, and as middle leaders, in partnership with senior management, we had begun to propel this change onward and forward.

# The play project and its key features – schema and loose parts

### The lens of schema

Whilst struggling to describe, and in turn add value to the fascinating child-led outdoor play that we observed in groups of children with SLD and autism, we had a lightbulb moment and discovered schema. This was the same group of children whose special interests, behaviours, and play were observed through a behaviourist lens and often described in terms of deficit language, like highly restrictive, repetitive, obsessive, and narrowly focused. We did not interpret what we saw in this way; we 'presumed competence' (Causton-Theoharis, 2014, p. 78). We saw their play in terms of strengths and something to be celebrated. Play that was often labelled in these limiting terms was in fact a *necessity* for the child. Their self-directed and self-initiated play often had a self-regulating and integrating effect and was 'deep and meaningful' (Bruce, 2012) for them.

The child with autism was not an empty vessel that needed filling with skills and adult-led experiences, much like the banking concept in Friere's 'Pedagogy of the Oppressed' (2017). This group of children did not experience anything like the play described by Bruce (2018) in her 12 features of free-flow play. She stated that play can be deeply solitary. It can be an integrating mechanism, that children choose to play and children keep control as they play. Historically, play for this group of children was adult-led and skills-based, with a goal in mind. It was not inclusive. In fact, what often started with good intentions was having an indirect discriminatory impact on children with autism, and their right to play and communicate in their own way was not being upheld or fully understood.

Looking through our newly acquired schematic lens enabled us to identify, nourish, and extend their play (Nutbrown, 2011).

## Schema: a definition

*'(persistent) pattern(s) of repeatable behaviour(s) into which experiences are assimilated and that are gradually coordinated. Co-ordinations lead to higher-level and more powerful schemas.'*

(Athey, 1990, p. 37)

## Some common schema and corresponding actions/behaviours

- **Trajectory** – climbing up, jumping down, dropping items from a height.
- **Positioning** – lining things up, placing them in groups.
- **Enveloping** – covering themselves/objects completely, wrapping up, placing in containers.
- **Rotating** – spinning self/objects, running around in circles/being swung around.
- **Enclosing** – adding boundaries to play areas, adding borders to pictures.
- **Transporting** – carrying/moving items from one place to another in containers or bags.
- **Connecting** – setting out and dismantling tracks, constructing, joining items with tape or glue.
- **Transforming** – exploring changing states of materials, transforming them from a solid to liquid and back again.
- **Orienteering** – positioning themselves/objects in different places or positions, for example upside down, on their side.

# Setting up the outdoors and indoors environment with loose parts

Each environment was furnished with 'loose parts', a term first referred to by Nicholson (2009) to describe materials/objects that can be used and moved in limitless ways. Nicholson introduced the idea that *we* are the experts when it comes to our learning environments, and we do not need other experts to tell us otherwise. This philosophy inspired us to create an outdoor area that gave the children a sense of agency – an environment that promoted choice, decision-making, and respect for the child's ideas and actions.

An understanding of the affordances of an environment, as seen by a child, is essential in providing an exciting setting for play (Tovey, 2007). Play settings are made up of affordances whereby real objects, and environments are given meaning by the person who perceives them. For example, a child perceiving a fallen tree as something upon which to climb and balance.

This is especially important for children on the autism spectrum, who will always find a novel affordance, not always obvious or valued by us neurotypicals.

Keeping all this in mind, we created a dynamic learning environment that reflected the children's dominant schema through its loose parts. For example, carpet rolls from the local carpet warehouse to roll, stand upright, tip over, roll, and carry; and rope to wiggle, pull, travel under, step over, and thread through.

Historically, classes would come to the outdoor area set up with loose parts. Most children would run outside with great enthusiasm, whilst some would just watch from a distance. The adults were unsure about their role outdoors and often used the time to observe, teach a skill, or model symbolic play. It was important for staff to realise that our children primarily engaged in sensory play and were not yet at the symbolic stage.

> We supported class teams to develop an interactionist approach by modelling the principles of Intensive Interaction to develop communication and the child's play. We also supported them to spot and record the children's schema and to extend/scaffold their play in the zone of proximal development (ZPD).

### Indoor lesson planning/organisation

To fine-tune support given to staff teams, we decided to go indoors where the space was smaller and where we felt more able to model and develop the FoCs through free-flow play.

We located a spare classroom, cleared it, found resources, and packed everything into good old IKEA bags ready to set up quickly at the start of a session. Lesson plans were carefully structured with a range of activities, staffing clearly deployed and directed, and resources to hand, using songs and rhymes to define key points during the session.

## Observations and assessment

Observing and assessing the children during the initial sessions showed they were mainly at a pre-symbolic level and mostly engaged in exploratory, sensory play, using all their senses to explore their environment. Their stage of social play was primarily solitary, but they were happy to play alongside each other.

> Observations of them at play and the way in which they played provided us with invaluable knowledge on how to tune in, connect, follow, and engage with our children to develop their play and communication.

During the first sessions we also observed each child's *developmental level of communication*. All children had a severe language delay and showed significant gaps in the FoCs, such as joint attention, imitation, requesting and turn-taking initiating interactions, the use and understanding of vocalisations, and eye contact. Without these fundamentals, the building blocks of all learning (Hewett, 2018), our children are not able to develop their emotional and learning potential and most importantly their human right and need to enjoy being with and engaging with another person (Hewett et al., 2019).

Video observations played a crucial role in the assessment process by providing a baseline, assessing progress over time, and reflecting upon our practice. The interaction between practitioner and child were looked at closely to discuss the effectiveness of the practitioner's style in nurturing the child's communication and play.

The Mandeville Developmental Curriculum and Assessment tool covers all aspects of early communication and reflects the development of the FoCs. In conjunction with our video case studies it was used effectively to assess a child's baseline and to show their progress over time.

## The role of the adult

As practitioners we supported the children in their social interactions and play using the communicative principles and processes of Intensive Interaction. We scaffolded their play sequences in the ZPD (see Chapter 4) – the gap that exists between what the child can do by themselves and what they can do with the support and guidance of an adult.

We really wanted the adults to have their own fun by playing and joining in with the children at their level. Some adults initially experienced difficulty in letting go of the 'teaching a skill' approach and were thus over-directive, whilst others saw their role as primarily one of watching and supervising.

As the weeks progressed the adults became more relaxed and began to play alongside the children, jumping in the puddles, playing in the mud, sharing a shelter, and sliding down the volcano side by side. As the adults let go of their inhibitions a more natural flow of communication developed.

Joining the child in their play also entailed having two of each material/object so that the adult could join in parallel, imitative play with the child, following and naturally modelling/scaffolding their play but not trying to teach specific skills (Wieder and Greenspan, 2003). We found it was best to accompany their play by a simple running commentary, not questions or instructions which demand an answer or a set way of doing something. Murphy (2012) advocated using declarative language as an invitation to interact, whereby we looked at the world together and commented upon what the child was doing from the child's perspective.

> Research findings show that imitative play is effective in increasing social interaction and intentional communication, such as looking, vocalising, requesting, smiling, and engaging in turn-taking play (Nind, 2005). The process of Intensive Interaction naturally facilitated and nurtured joint attention by following the child's lead and tuning in with their communicative intent and play.
>
> There is no fixed way of organising your team in a free-flow play environment. Reflection and flexibility are the key ingredients to success. We chose not to assign particular adults to particular areas or children so as to create a more flexible, responsive environment.

## Case study 1: Judah

### Profile and description

Judah has a diagnosis of SLD and autism, epilepsy, a visual impairment, and pica (craving and eating non-food materials). He was seven years old at the time of the project and able to express basic needs and emotions through vocalisations. Judah was a sociable boy who would sometimes express delight by rushing towards people. These enthusiastic initiations often resulted in his peers being knocked over.

When walking, Judah held his body stiffly to maintain his balance. This way of walking, along with a need to feel the sensory sensation of 'tipping and teetering' on any raised ledges (tables, windowsills), meant Judah required close supervision to explore his environment safely. This often resulted in his explorations being curtailed. By week two of our project his own dynamic risk assessment came into play which offered freedom with safety!

### Description of a dynamic movement–based sequence with Judah within the free-flow indoor classroom

'Communicating and playing together is like dancing together, people have to tune into each other, to be sensitive to what others do and respond appropriately' (Bruce, 2018, p. 11).

In the middle of the classroom, Judah had chosen to lay on the floor and juggle with a hoop. Prior to this he had been exploring corn flour and water. Other activities within the room were sand play and carpet roll play.

I began to **observe** Judah and decided to **complement** Judah's actions and not directly copy his juggling.

I **tuned in** and in identifying Judah's **rotation** and **trajectory** schema, decided to circle (**rotation**) round him, with a stamping action (**trajectory**) all within his **ZPD**. What evolved was a dynamic sequence of communication and movement that resembled a dance.

I added a 'Stamp! Stamp! Stamp!' (**reciprocal language – RL**) commentary to accompany my action. Whilst Judah continued to juggle the hoop, he smiled and tracked my movement.

Judah then miraculously began to **join me in my sequence** by stamping his feet *whilst* juggling!

As I **tuned in, the right moment to develop** and **acknowledge** Judah's action and **connection with me** presented itself. I exclaimed: 'Judah stamping!' (**RL**), at which point Judah threw down his hoop and got up off the floor.

As Judah got up, I had a moment to **pause** and consciously **ease back** on my movement, only then to 'pop in' an emotionally charged, but staggered, 'Ready . . . steady . . . GO!' I built the anticipation through my body language and voice, which kept him engaged, and through my responses we gradually developed the flow and the content of the activity together.

We managed to repeat this sequence twice with two additions: an onlooking peer joined us with no collisions! And Judah began to move across the space (**trajectory**).

Judah brought our sequence to a natural end, and however tempting it was for me to continue this lively dance, I honoured his decision.

We had created a funny little world. It was hilarious and so wonderful to be a part of. Judah had taken **control** of the sequence; he'd moved his body creatively whilst keeping his balance and maintained control without knocking anyone over. He demonstrated that given the right circumstances, he could get really excited and bring himself down to a calm, contented state, drawing the dance to a close.

And the best thing about the sequence? We could never have planned for it! It was a unique, priceless moment in time. And to my surprise, the following week Judah briefly initiated the dance again! This interaction, where I became the 'loose part' for Judah, was to be a pivotal moment in our relationship. Each week our playful bond continued to develop as his FoCs emerged, and with loose parts linked to his schema Judah continued to reveal to us all that he could do.

## Summary of Judah's progress in the FoCs and techniques used to make that progress possible

| Which FoCs did Judah learn during the play sessions? | What Intensive Interaction techniques was the adult using? |
|---|---|
| I am listened to. | They let Judah lead the interaction. |
| I am respected. | They paused for him to respond. |
| I am liked and you like what I do. | They honoured and respected his decision-making. |
| I can have fun and I am fun to be with. I can share fun. | They had fun. |
| I have a friend and other people are good to be with. | They were totally tuned in to Judah. |
| Other people like my games. | They showed him how much they love to play with him. |
| I can coordinate a rhythmic stamp and practise my hand–eye coordination | They enjoyed his play and company. |
| I can take control and repeat things I like. | They had confidence in him. |
| I am learning to regulate my emotions. | They gave him time and support to do this. |

**Figure 9.1** Case study: Judah – progress in the Fundamentals of Communication and techniques used.

# Case study 2: Tanzeela

## Profile and description

Tanzeela has autism and SLD and has not yet developed speech. At the time of the project, she was five years old and understood a few key phrases said in context.

Tanzeela was wrapped up in her own little world and very anxious about venturing out into any different environments. Transitions were difficult for her. She did not initiate many interactions with any of the adults around her.

### Initial observations

Tanzeela observed from a distance and chose not to come into the main play area. We respected this. She practised her **trajectory** schema and liked to **envelop** herself in fabric and go under the table (**enclosure**). We took the loose parts over to Tanzeela to match her previously observed schema (**enclosure** and **trajectory** – wooden planks, leaves, and a cardboard shelter). In doing so, we created a learning environment where she felt emotionally secure and safe to learn.

### Progress observed in Tanzeela's bespoke free-flow area

- **Tanzeela really noticed me for the first time!**

I joined-in with Tanzeela by walking repeatedly backwards and forwards along the wall (**trajectory schema**). I decided to take over some wooden planks to make two pathways, one for her and one for me (extending the learning in her ZPD). Tanzeela took up the suggestion, and we walked up and down our individual paths. This game captured her attention and concentration for the entire 15-minute session.

- **Tanzeela shared an activity with another person.**

We sat in the large cardboard box shelter together (**enclosure**) just happily being together, glancing at each other and exchanging smiles as we both played with the holey, plastic balls we had stuck on our fingers. Tanzeela vocalised as we played, and I vocalised back. We banged the balls together in a tapping game, swapping them from hand to hand and between each other.

## Progress observed in the indoor free-flow classroom

- **Tanzeela initiated an interaction.**

I positioned myself at a distance, tuned-in and available. Tanzeela glanced over occasionally as she skipped backwards and forwards (***trajectory***). After 5 minutes Tanzeela ran towards me, grasped my hands, and clapped them together whilst placing her face very close to mine. She did this several times smiling, looking, and stroking my hair.

- **Tanzeela played a turn-taking game with me for the first time.**

The following week, Katy worked with Tanzeela. She introduced a large carpet roll, a fabulous loose part that would potentially complement Tanzeela's ***trajectory*** schema. Katy **waited** several minutes before Tanzeela decided to join her in the roll play. They had a great time playing a 'Ready, Steady, BOING!' game of Tanzeela knocking the roll down as Katy popped it back up again. During the pause Tanzeela vocalised and looked at the fallen roll to ask for more.

- **Tanzeela's repertoire of activities developed over time.**

Tanzeela picked up one end of the carpet roll, and we looked at each other through either end. What fun we had playing our new game of I Spy! I introduced one of her favourite balls, and together we created a new game of rolling the ball down the carpet roll to each other. We varied the game by standing up and both trying to retrieve the ball at the same time – Tanzeela's idea. These magical moments were perfectly captured on video and are an absolute joy to watch. They capture perfectly Tanzeela's learning journey and progress over time.

## Summary of Tanzeela's progress in the FoCs and techniques used to make that progress possible

| Which FoCs did Tanzeela learn during the play sessions? | What Intensive Interaction techniques was the adult using? |
|---|---|
| I can use and understand eye contact and vocalisations. | We were unhurried, relaxed, and responsive. |
| I can make up my own game. | We followed Tanzeela's lead. |
| I can attend to another person. | We allowed her to be in the lead. |
| I can play a fun turn-taking game. | We enjoyed playing too. |
| I can ask you to play with me. | We tuned in and really listened to Tanzeela. |
| I can choose and lead my own play. | We became Tanzeela's plaything and play partner. |
| I can enjoy being with another person. | We paused and waited effectively. |
| I can share personal space. | We didn't do too much. |
| I can ask for more. | We celebrated Tanzeela's wow moments. |
| I can copy you and I know when you are copying me. | We reflected on learning outcomes by looking at video observations after each session. |
| I can share attention and look at something at the same time as you. | We reflected on where Tanzeela's learning journey might go next. |

**Figure 9.2** Case study: Tanzeela – progress in the Fundamentals of Communication and techniques used.

## Evaluation of our research project

Our project sought to challenge the idea that children with autism and SLD struggle to play in a free-flow environment and that they often become absorbed and stuck in repetitive behaviours. Many of these are the repetitive actions of schematic play which allowed our children the freedom to construct meaning in what they were doing and to regulate their sensory processing difficulties. Also, by joining a child in their repetitive behaviours, a door can be opened to connecting with the child in a respectful and meaningful way, thus nurturing their development of the FoCs.

The learning environment both indoors and outdoors provided the best conditions for the process of Intensive Interaction to emerge and grow. There was a naturally occurring flow to the play and interactions between children and adults. At times both were so deeply engaged the sense of time disappeared (Csikszentmihalyi, 1990). Both Intensive Interaction and free-flow play are well-suited partners. They meld and mould to become one to the point where we are unable to say whether we are playing or doing Intensive Interaction.

The dynamic environment we created with loose parts and the children's schema in mind afforded multi-dimensional play possibilities; play possibilities that we adults do not always recognise (Tovey, 2007). The children were in control of their play and their environment.

> The loose parts often provided a reason to communicate and a starting point for Intensive Interaction. They provided a way in for the adult to tune in and connect with the child. They can also be used at a sensory, functional, or symbolic level to reflect the developmental stage of the child, therefore not restricting the competence of the child.

Video case studies showed very clear progress in communication and play for all the children involved. This progress could in turn be mapped on their individual assessment on our developmental curriculum. Our video case studies were powerful in providing evidence that free-flow play, alongside Intensive Interaction, was effective in engaging our children and developing their FoCs.

## Concluding remarks

We now embrace a Froebelian approach/pedagogy enhanced by the Intensive Interaction principles and techniques – an approach that is based on sound theory and research, where play is celebrated as the child's work and is considered to be the highest form of learning. Truly connecting with the child to create trusting, secure relationships is also at the heart of all that we do.

Taking the path of freedom was not always easy, but without freedom there is no autonomy, and without autonomy there can be no meaningful learning. Within our autonomous free-flow play environments the children were free to show us what they knew, and the adults were free to tune in, celebrate, and honour the child's gifts. Together we developed their play and their FoCs, facilitating their learning potential and nurturing their emotional well-being.

## References

Anderson, M. (2007). *Tales from the Table: Lovaas/ABA Intervention with Children on the Autistic Spectrum*. London: Jessica Kingsley.

Athey, C. (1990). *Extending Thought in Young Children: A Parent-Teacher Partnership*. London: Paul Chapman.

Bruce, T. (2012). *Early Childhood Practice*. London: Sage Publishing.

Bruce, T. (2018). *Early Childhood Education*. 5th ed. London: Hodder Education.

Causton-Theoharis, J. (2014). *The Paraprofessional's Handbook for Effective Support in Inclusive Classrooms*. New York: Brookes Publishing.

Csikszentmihalyi, M. (1990). *Flow: The Psychology of Optimal Experience*. New York: Harper and Row.

Department for Education, (2017). *Statutory Framework for the Early Years Foundation Stage: Setting the Standards for Learning, Development and Care for Children from Birth to Five*. Available at: https://assets.publishing.service.gov.uk/government/uploads/system/uploads/attachment_data/file/596629/EYFS_STATUTORY_FRAMEWORK_2017.pdf [Accessed 25 February 2021].

Friere, P. (2017). *Pedagogy of the Oppressed*. London, UK: Penguin Random House.

Hewett, D. (2018). *The Intensive Interaction Handbook*. 2nd ed. London: Sage Publications.

Hewett, D., Calveley, J., McKim, J. and Mourière, A. (2019). Communication, human rights and Intensive Interaction. *PMLD Link*, 31(1), Issue 92, pp. 8–10.

Murphy, L. (2012). *Declarative Language by RDIconnect Communicating, RDI® Core Concepts*. Available at: www.rdiconnect.com/declarative-language [Accessed 19 February 2021].

Nicholson, S. (2009). The theory of loose parts: An important principle for design methodology. *Studies in Design Education Craft and Technology*, 4(2). Available at: https://ons.lboro.ac.uk/SDEC/article/view/1204> [Accessed 16 February 2021].

Nind, M. (2005). *Developing the Basics of Communication with People with SLD*. 2nd ed. London: David Fulton.

Nind, M. and Hewett, D. (1994). *Access to Communication: Developing the Basics of Communication for People Who Have Severe Learning Disabilities Through Intensive Interaction*. Abingdon: David Fulton.

Nutbrown, C. (2011). *Threads of Thinking: Schema and Young Children Learning*. 4th ed. London: Sage Publications.

Tovey, H. (2007). *Playing Outdoors: Spaces and Places, Risk and Challenge*. Maidenhead: Open University Press/McGraw-Hill Education.

Vygotsky, L. S. (1978). *Mind in Society*. Los Angeles, CA: University of California Press.

Wieder, S. and Greenspan, S. I. (2003). Climbing the symbolic ladder in the DIR model through floor time/interactive play. *Autism*, 7(4), pp. 425–435.

Yates, E. (2018). 'Play'. In: J. Johnston, L. Nahmad-Williams, R. Oates and V. Wood, eds., *Early Childhood Studies: Principles and Practice*, 2nd ed. Abingdon: Routledge, pp. 348–368.

# 10. Intensive Interaction and the birth of process-central curriculum access

*Sue Lowry and Bec Anderson*

Process-central curriculum access (PCCA) was a journey of discovery, grounded in Intensive Interaction but one that led us into new and unexpected terrain. As Intensive Interaction practitioners, we saw in our students their engagement, obvious communicative development, emotional and social understanding, and growth. These students were blossoming in the quality of their relationships – for some this meant to notice others, to share space and attention, and for others this led to the ability to now maintain relationships with their family. We are also classroom teachers in Australia, charged with the responsibility of delivering a mandated curriculum. The frustration of trying to adapt a content-laden mainstream curriculum for this same cohort of learners, and knowing we were doing it badly, led us to question our practice. If a student-led approach such as Intensive Interaction could work so incredibly well for communication, surely focusing on process rather than content was a place to start.

We began by looking to trusted sources for guidance. We looked to Imray and Hinchcliffe and their concept of process-based learning as a holistic approach rather than teaching to specific targeted objectives. For the teacher the process of learning becomes the objective; however, the learner decides where the process will go, the pace and direction of the learning, and therefore the pace and direction of the teaching. The teacher may prompt and try different strategies to elicit progress but will ultimately be guided to the learning outcome by the student (Imray and Hinchcliffe, 2014). This encapsulated the ethos of what we were trying to achieve. Was this going to be the way to deliver our mandated curriculum, with integrity for ourselves and meaning and purpose for our students? We needed to delve into these ideas further and flesh out how we could make this work in our classrooms.

> We went back to basics – how do children learn, and how do we teach? The fundamentals of learning are not taught to neurotypical children in the first year of life, they are enabled and allowed to grow through social play (Imray and Hinchcliffe, 2014). Bruner (1966) states that learning is an active process in which ideas or concepts develop based upon the current and past knowledge of the learner. Vygotsky (1978) and Hobson (2002) view social engagement as central to the origin of symbolic thinking and cognitive development. Rogoff (1990) contends that children learn through a cognitive apprenticeship while doing activities with more skilled partners, not through direct instruction. Could this be the same for students with a disability?

DOI: 10.4324/9781003170839-10

So it appeared to us that a process-based learning approach may have validity. This was reflected in the pedagogical response of constructionism (Harel and Papert, 1991), which advocates for student-centred discovery learning where students use information they already know to acquire more knowledge. The teacher's role is not that of a lecturer but a facilitator. What type of facilitator were we going to be?

We knew from our reading that learning had to be scaffolded (Bruner, 1966) and within the child's zone of proximal development (ZPD – Vygotsky, 1978). However, scaffolding in education is often seen as providing the structure for students to reach a designated target. If we were going to be student and process led, this conventional idea of scaffolding would not work. We came across the concept of soft scaffolding (Saye and Brush, 2002), and this, along with Rogoff's concept of a cognitive apprenticeship, were our lightbulb moments.

## Creating soft scaffolds

We began to explore the concept of a soft scaffold – a scaffold that could support the process of learning, rather than the learning of specific content. A scaffold which is an optimal but malleable learning environment that moves and changes with the learner.

Through discussions about how to create this reactive, social, accessible, and almost magical platform for learning, the imagery of a magic carpet was born.

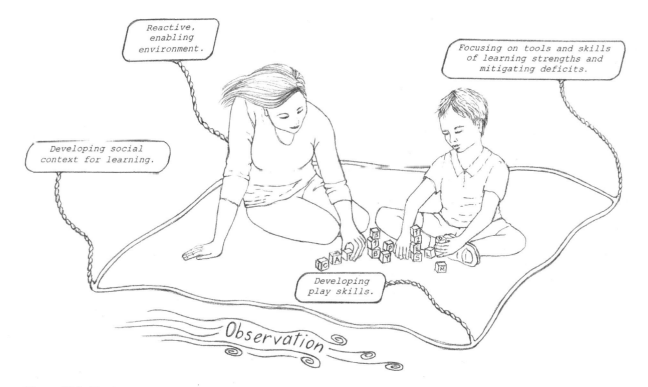

**Figure 10.1** Magic carpet.

The magic carpet itself is the optimal learning environment for the student. Just as in Intensive Interaction, the power of social interaction as a vehicle for learning meant that the ride on the magic carpet was not one that a student could take by themselves. But how to get the carpet to fly under the weight of the teacher, the child, and the curriculum?

Firstly, just as in Intensive Interaction, it must be powered and borne along by observation. We found that the teacher can maintain the balance and stability of the ride by using four main supporting strategies – developing a social context for learning, creating reactive enabling environments, focusing on learning strengths and mitigating deficits, and developing play skills. The use of supporting strategies will be differently tensioned for each student – for example, a student with significant physical impairments may require more time and thought into their reactive enabling environment support, while a student with autism may require their supports to be more focused in the social contexts and developing of their play skills.

## A practical guide to magic carpets and soft scaffolds

In this section, we will detail how to get the carpet flying, starting first with initial observations before discussing the creation of reactive enabling environments and how to develop play skills. We are focusing on reactive enabling environments and play skills because these are a concrete place to begin. As you work through this process, you will expand and develop your skills in creating social contexts for learning, as well as focusing on your students' strengths and mitigating their learning deficits.

### Observation

Observation always begins with the student, observing for the following:

- Preferences for objects or activities.
- Student strengths, likes, and interests.
- Links to possible underlying schema.
- Possibilities in all areas – often when our students are up to mischief, they show the extent of their skills and talents!

> Observation should be used as your starting point, your finishing point, and at all points in between. Fisher (2016) offers three important 'W's' for great observation – wait, watch, and wonder!

## Reactive enabling environments

At the centre of our work, we must take the approach of building the environment around the student, rather than plonking the student into an environment. Points to start with:

- The student's physical access – which muscles does the student have reliable, voluntary control over? Students should have the opportunity to be able to physically interact with and manipulate their learning environment. This access may not be with their hands – it could be with their feet or their left elbow. For students with the greatest physical impairment, sometimes the removal of gravity (through suspending them or materials they are working with or floating in water) can provide physical access.
- We need to cater to the sensory channels the student has available to them – their dominant sense may not be visual. Prioritising the visual is a trap of the sighted.
- The learning environment needs to be flexible – are you able to set up, change, and pack away with ease?
- Consider the true range of learning opportunities available within the environment – often the simplest things (such as a cardboard box) can be the most versatile and valuable learning tools.
- The learning environment may get destroyed by the student during use – if it is expensive or Pinterest-worthy, it could inhibit how you let the student work within the space. Think extremely robust or extremely expendable.
- Does the student have agency over their own learning? Students must be active participants – passive watching of other people doing things or passively watching the environment is not enough.
- If your observations have seen strong evidence of developing or exploration of schema, are there opportunities for that to extend?

Once you have considered these points, you must ensure there are opportunities for social interaction in every environment. Are there opportunities for shared attention, anticipatory games and turn-taking?

If you are providing opportunities for social interaction, and the student is forming concepts about how the world works around them, then you are creating the environment for early communication about concepts. This early communication does not have to be verbal – it can be as simple as sharing the recognition of change, difference, or enjoyment.

## Developing play skills

According to Stagnitti (1998, p. VI), '*The child's success in play is vital to their development of language, social and cognitive skills*'. Unfortunately, what characterises our students most is a lack of play skills, in particular, understanding the social aspect of play and the skill of playing with others. This can be further compounded by the idiosyncratic nature of their interests, which may fall far from the general play paradigms of the neurotypical. In the previous section, we discussed the debilitating effect that being unable to physically access the world around you has on the ability to learn. This also pertains to developing play skills.

Again, we went back to looking at trusted sources. Vygotsky and the ZPD (1978) seemed an obvious place to start. However, how do you lock in to where that zone actually is and develop play skills within it? Rogoff's work on cognitive apprenticeships (1990) – the idea that children learn while doing activities with more-skilled partners, not through direct instruction – also makes specific mention to the valuable role of siblings and other children as the more skilled partners. Due to the idiosyncratic nature of our students' play paradigms, the spontaneous cognitive apprenticeship that usually develops between children does not generally occur.

> Intensive Interaction takes the infant/caregiver model and analyses and hones it to create the social ecology for developing the Fundamentals of Communication (FoCs). We started thinking about how close siblings, who are 12–18 months apart in age, start to develop a cognitive apprenticeship through their natural play. Could we identify and hone our skills to create a social ecology for developing play skills?

In observing the play of neurotypical siblings that were close in age, we noted that often the older sibling would be slightly more skilled while retaining all the joy and enthusiasm in all the same play topics. Could we fulfil that role within the idiosyncratic play paradigms of our students? As we started to think about this, we gave it the shorthand title of a 'Close Sibling Model'. To do this well, we needed to follow the student's agenda and play topics, gently interrupt habitual play (but remain within the same play topic), introduce moments of playful tension, look for opportunities to increase challenge, and where possible, foster collaboration between students. As we continued to refine our technique, it became apparent that getting the cognitive apprenticeship working is not child's play – it requires skilled and attuned professionals.

As we moved on this path, we were walking the tightrope between remaining student-led and avoiding becoming motivated by our teacher agendas. This line that we walk and where the boundaries are was clarified for us by the work of Fisher (2016). Her studies in mainstream nurseries and early-years settings found that in adult-led learning, practitioners focus children's thinking; in adult-initiated learning, practitioners fathom children's learning; and in child-led learning, practitioners follow children's thinking.

Neurotypical learners are quite robust; we found our students to be far more fragile in their skills as a learner, easily disengaging in adult-led and adult-initiated learning. Therefore, to ensure engagement, we must start and be rooted in following the student's agenda. When we are ready to slightly extend using the Close Sibling Model, we are both following and gently trying to fathom the depth and breadth of their learning. And ultimately, when the student is comfortable working right at the edge of their ZPD, practitioners can focus a student's thinking to move in new and novel directions. If you begin at the adult-led learning level, you lose the students who are not confident, secure, autonomous learners, and the curriculum becomes a collection of disengaging activities.

## Pedagogy meets curriculum

> Now you have your magic carpet up and flying, and your supports appropriately tensioned for each student for optimal learning. How do you use it to navigate the travails of the mandated curriculum?

If you are given the task of taking a mainstream curriculum, adapting it for students with special needs, and you focus on the content, you are failing to recognise the extreme fragility of our students as learners. These learners are still working on building the cognitive sub-structures, which are the massive developments in the brain that underpin cognitive development and all other learning. These students are still learning how to learn. Therefore, the focus has to be on building a cognitive apprenticeship. If you are not certain of what a cognitive apprenticeship is and how to develop it, it is easy to go off the rails into tokenism.

> To facilitate a cognitive apprenticeship, we need to consider what the student and the staff are bringing to the learning. For students, this may include mastered and emergent skills, their current knowledge and understanding of the world, and their previous successes and failures as learners. For staff, this must include a process-central pedagogical approach, such as Intensive Interaction, underpinned by extensive knowledge of early learning. This is the knowledge base we use to tension the four supports of each student's magic carpet. If we do this well, the student never notices what we are doing and develops their skills as learners while being engaged in meaningful activities with a responsive partner. This leads to a meeting of minds in a reactive enabling environment – this is a cognitive apprenticeship.

The depth of knowledge required cannot be covered within a single book chapter. A good place to start is with the work of Staves (2001, 2019). This will give you a good grounding in early cognitive development and schema and provide a good springboard for further reading.

Getting a cognitive apprenticeship right was the hardest task of all. We were engaged as learners ourselves in the course of action research to develop our ideas, and in the process realised that each of our students had become an action research project in their own right.

# The 1–5–3 sub-structure of process-central curriculum access

The action research model – of observing and collecting data, evaluating the data, reflecting, planning and making provisions, and then acting – provided the structure for how we could articulate our planning process within the curriculum context. Thus, the 1–5–3 sub-structure of PCCA was created. A case study of Tilda will illustrate the 1–5–3 sub-structure in action.

**One student** – everything is centred around the student and your observations of their strengths, capacity, and agency. Every phase relates to them and is driven by them.

**Five phases** of the process – the idea phase, the planning phase, the learning phase, the emergent outcome phase, and the assessment phase.

**Three key elements** of implementation within each phase.

As the student is central to this model, observation is the driving force, and within each of these phases we will outline the types and depth of observation required.

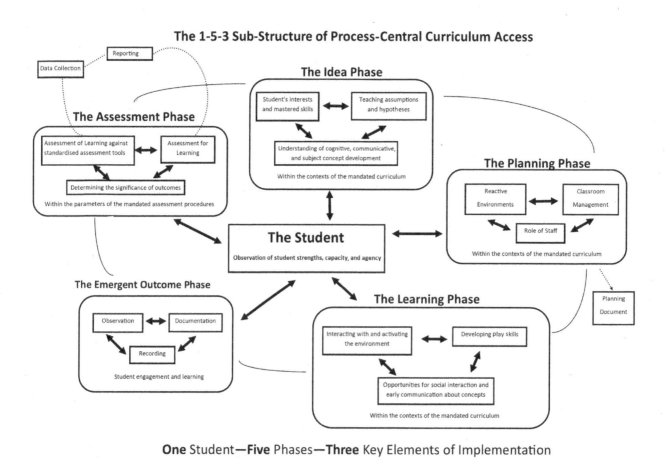

Figure 10.2 1–5–3 sub-structure of process-central curriculum access.

## The idea phase

In this phase, the three key elements of implementation are:

- The student's interests and mastered skills.
- The teacher's underpinning knowledge of cognitive, communicative, and early subject concept development.
- Any assumptions and hypotheses that may have arisen from the initial observations coupled with teacher underpinning knowledge.

In this phase, we also have to consider – do these assumptions provide a clear link to the curriculum through evidence of early subject concept development? Do they illuminate clear patterns in the student's actions that could provide a portal through which we can fly the magic carpet into other curriculum areas?

## The planning phase

In this phase, the three key elements of implementation are:

- Reactive environments.
- The role of the staff.
- Classroom management.

This phase requires questioning all previous observations to begin developing a repertoire of learning opportunities as a starting point. Even though you are working on early developmental concepts, some materials have a 'flavour' of a particular curriculum area (Staves, 2001) – for example, art may give rise to exploring art materials, colour, light, and shape, and in music, sound, vibration, pulse, and pattern. This must be done sensitively, and it must always be remembered that it is the process of learning which is important, not the finished product. This cohort is generally developing the fundamental underpinnings of cognition and communication, rather than any specific subject knowledge.

When devising and creating reactive enabling environments you must consider a range of contexts for exploration. As long as you're staying within each student's ZPD, the discipline of giving students access to the mandated curriculum can prove for staff a stimulus for creative thinking. For students, this can provide broad and rich contexts in which to learn.

How can you insert yourself into these environments with the student while remaining student led? How do you create a cognitive apprenticeship? How do we use the Close Sibling Model to develop play skills and provide opportunities for communication about early concept development? While repetition is good, enforced habituation is not so good! Offer repetition of learning environments with opportunities for variation and scope for further development. Staff could offer a variety of multi-purpose materials, such as large boxes, cardboard tubes, and buckets that can be used in a variety of ways. In this element, patience is required! It can take several sessions before a student feels secure and confident enough to explore different reactive environments and materials. It may also take staff time to work out how to sensitively join the play to create a productive social ecology.

> From questioning your observations and your knowledge of cognitive, communicative, and subject development, you have planned and refined the soft scaffold you are building for this student. However, we are classroom teachers, and we may have five or six students (or more!) who are all working on different concepts. How do you organise your classroom to manage this?

From our experiences, there are several ways the classroom can be structured that have worked for us. Three possible options are cross-curricula installations, subject-related workstations, and highly individualised classrooms.

- **Cross-curricula installations**

This way of working was developed by teachers working with students in their first years of schooling. Literacy and numeracy opportunities are interwoven throughout sensory environments which invite exploration. The environments, which are changed daily, are based on observations of student interests and offer multiple opportunities for concept development – such as early numeracy, early literacy, concepts of print, and environments that are catered to students' sensory interests. There is a fluidity in the day; however, time and space are given for independent and shared exploration, including Intensive Interaction input. When the students arrive in the morning, they are invited to explore the room. The staff look for opportunities to join the students in their play. When the soft scaffolds are tailored effectively, each child will be riding their magic carpet as they work on their 'big picture' learning – their cognitive, communicative, social, and emotional development.

- **Subject-related workstations**

This way of working was developed in the upper primary and secondary sectors of the school. The focus remains on developing the cognitive apprenticeship; however, throughout the day, the magic carpet flies through different curriculum areas – such as maths, English, and science. This provides the opportunity for staff to resource and offer a variety and breadth of learning contexts and reactive enabling environments. In practice, this involves a station-style set up with a curriculum area focus, such as maths. Across the school day, students may explore three different curriculum areas using stations. There would be one station per student based on observed idiosyncratic interests, strengths, and/or observed schema. In addition, there is usually a 'wildcard' station, based on the educated guesswork of staff in the room, to provide a new experience that may capture the interest of the students. Students have access to all the stations and can move freely between them. Even though this model has more subject structure than the cross-curricula model, it must be noted that all staff working in these classrooms are fully trained in Intensive Interaction. Intensive Interaction opportunities continue regardless of the stations that are set up. Taskless times are also worked into the day where Intensive Interaction is given top priority.

- **Highly individualised classrooms**

The greater the physical needs of the students, the more individualised each learning environment needs to be in order to create access and agency for that student. This way of working is most suitable for students with profound and multiple learning difficulties (PMLD). There are countless books written about creating reactive environments for learners with PMLD. However, they often focus on cause and effect in the environment and may not offer or consider opportunities for co-exploration and shared attention. Without sharing the environment with a play partner, these students do not have the opportunity to develop the skills of learning from others through a cognitive apprenticeship.

Regardless of the model or combination of models you choose, a successful classroom is dependent on the process being student led but teacher managed.

## The learning phase

In this phase, the three key elements of implementation are:

- Interacting with and activating the environment.
- Developing play skills.
- Opportunities for social interaction and early communication about concepts.

> When working with the student, you must be responding to your observations both in the moment as well as storing away information for further reflection. These are some of the questions to ask yourself during this phase. Am I following the student's lead? Am I pushing my own agenda? Am I seeing any change in the student's actions or behaviour? How can I follow, subtly extend, or capitalise on this? Does what is happening feel or look significant? Video! If you can't video, write it down.

Can the reactive environment be modified to better suit the student? Can I link what they are doing now to something I have seen them doing previously? Are there opportunities to join the student in play? Are there obvious links to early maths schema, stages of play, cognitive or communicative development? Video! Write it down!

## The emergent outcome phase

In this phase, the three key elements of implementation are:

- Observation.
- Documentation.
- Recording.

The use of observation in this phase must work hand in glove with the learning phase. Trying to be vigilant of what is significant and videoing or documenting it in the learning phase is the ideal; however, careful analysis of video, written documentation, or student artefacts is where the emergent outcomes will be found. Knowing and being able to identify the FoCs; early communicative, cognitive, and symbolic development; early maths schema; etc. is vital to being able to observe and then record or document emergent outcomes.

We need to recognise and value horizontal as well as vertical progress. Never ignore something significant just because it does not appear on a formal assessment tool. This may be vital for building future learning for that student. Be systematic about recording and then storing these observations.

## The assessment phase

In this phase, the three key elements of implementation are:

- Determining the significance of outcomes.
- Assessment of learning against standardised assessment tools.
- Assessment for learning.

Individual governments and local education authorities will dictate assessment tools and reporting procedures. The most important thing is using the large body of knowledge you have about this student to inform your observations of what they are currently doing and starting the process all over again. The 1–5–3 continues forward.

## Tilda: a case study

Tilda was an eight-year-old student with whom we were using Intensive Interaction. She was non-verbal and beginning to engage in social interactions with staff. Observations of Tilda in her classroom environment revealed that she would sit in the ball pit and repeatedly pick up and drop balls. As staff continued to observe her across the school day, this action was noted in another context – picking up and dropping her rice at lunch. Using our knowledge of early development, it appeared to be related to the schema of trajectory.

This was an obvious link to early mathematics concepts. Could the action and the context of dropping and falling be used as a way of accessing science or art?

The class staff looked at what the mandated curriculum required to be covered, the observations of Tilda, and how we could develop that and her communicative skills to get a cognitive apprenticeship rolling within those curriculum contexts.

Tilda's classroom used the subject-related workstations model. Staff planned workstations based on Tilda's observed interest in dropping and falling objects. For maths, the curriculum required early number sense, specifically exploring and counting small quantities (0–3). Using knowledge of early maths, staff recognised that Tilda required the ability to share attention and sustain mutual focus on objects to be able to develop later skills, such as counting. To foster this social connectedness in her solitary activities, staff planned to join her in her ball pit play. For art, the curriculum required colour mixing, so the team planned a paint bomb dropping station. For science, the curriculum required exploration and creation of simple machines, so the team planned a station with materials to create ball runs.

Working in the learning phase with Tilda, staff began with parallel play. Tilda began to take notice of the staff and appeared intrigued. Over time and many repeated play sessions, staff were able to use the Close Sibling Model to develop a series of simple anticipatory games using the language, 'One, two, three . . . Go!' During maths, staff used earlier observations of Tilda playing with rice as inspiration to set up a sensory rice play station. Over a ten-week period, the previously non-verbal Tilda started saying, 'Go!' to indicate she wanted the staff member to drop the rice. She then began preceding this with 'One, two, three. . .' which was later extended to alternating counts to ten aloud with a staff member! In art, Tilda went from avoiding art activities to being actively and enthusiastically engaged. In science, she not only built her own simple ball runs but was reaching out to indicate when she needed the assistance of staff and looking to their faces for a reaction as the ball emerged.

## Emergent outcomes

Tilda's progress was documented through systematic videoing and note taking by class staff. By analysing the video, emergent outcomes were identified, including:

- Developing and using problem-solving skills.
- Understanding sequences and developing increasingly sophisticated sequences.
- Developing early concepts of size, such as big and small.
- Rehearsing the sequence of number names through counting games and activities.

- Developing shared attention in activities.
- Developing concentration and attention span.
- Taking turns.
- Using and understanding eye contact and facial expressions.
- Learning use and understanding of vocalisations, having vocalisations become more varied and extensive, then gradually more precise and meaningful – leading to the development of speech.
- Using and understanding non-verbal communication.
- Enjoying being with another person.

In subsequent years, following this PCCA approach and plenty of Intensive Interaction input, Tilda developed the ability to speak in context about topics that fascinated her. She selected, organised, and sang nursery rhymes around the theme of falling. She learned to read and spell and began to develop imaginative play with objects and people. She began organising staff and fellow students into increasingly complex social games that involved as many people as possible falling down around her. Most recently, she is using AAC to communicate on a much broader range of topics. The trajectory schema, which proved the key for us entering Tilda's world, still appears to be a driving force in her communicative and cognitive development.

## Concluding remarks

In the 1980s in Australia there was a breast cancer awareness campaign featuring Rembrandt's *Bathsheba*. The premise of the campaign was that most people will look at the painting and see a woman bathing. An oncologist will look at the painting and see breast cancer. As we worked through the process of developing PCCA, we realised the depth and breadth of knowledge that we needed to gain to see beneath the surface of our students' actions.

By extending our knowledge base and questioning our practice, we developed a pedagogical approach which was born out of Intensive Interaction but in turn became an overarching environment in which Intensive Interaction flourished. As we and our students set off on our magic carpet ride, we discovered that when teachers can change the way they think about teaching, students can change the way they think about learning.

## References

Bruner, J. (1966). *Toward a Theory of Instruction*. New York: W. W. Norton and Company.

Fisher, J. (2016). *Interacting or Interfering? Improving Interactions in the Early Years*. Maidenhead: Open University Press.

Harel, I. and Papert, S. (1991). *Constructionism*. Norwood, NJ: Ablex Publishing.

Hobson, P. (2002). *The Cradle of Thought: Exploring the Origins of Thinking*. London: Pan Macmillan.

Imray, P. and Hinchcliffe, V. (2014). *Curricula for Teaching Children and Young People with Severe or Profound and Multiple Learning Difficulties; Practical Strategies for Educational Professionals*. London: Routledge.

Rogoff, B. (1990). *Apprenticeship in Thinking; Cognitive Development in Social Context*. Oxford: Oxford University Press.

Saye, J. and Brush, T. (2002). A summary of research exploring hard and soft scaffolding for teachers and students using a multimedia supported learning environment. *The Journal of Interactive Online Learning*, 1(2), pp. 1–11.

Stagnitti, K. (1998). *Learn to Play – A Practical Program to Develop a Child's Imaginative Play Skills*. Victoria, Australia: Co-Ordinates Publications.

Staves, L. (2001). *Mathematics for Children with Severe and Profound Learning Difficulties*. London: David Fulton Publishers Ltd.

Staves, L. (2019). *Very Special Maths; Developing Thinking and Maths Skills for Pupils with Severe or Complex Learning Difficulties*. London: Routledge.

Vygotsky, L. S. (1978). *Mind in Society: The Development of Psychological Processes*. Cambridge, MA: Harvard University Press.

# 11. Touch
## The cement that binds us

*Julia Barnes*

As a teacher of children with PMLD, I use touch in most interactions with my pupils. Although I have worked less frequently with pupils with SLD and autism, I do not think I have ever participated in Intensive Interaction with a person that has not involved a touchpoint. For some, this involves gentle touch, tickles, clapping, and tapping, whilst others prefer deeper pressures, such as leaning, resting, squeezing, or even sitting on/being sat on! Sometimes all-encompassing hugs which block out the rest of the world and make sure you are in the moment together. In my view touch is not an icing-on-the-cake luxury, it is fundamentally far deeper, it is the cement that binds us.

In this chapter, I will explore some of the physiological, psychological, and sociological implications of touch for humans and then consider why it may be especially pertinent to Intensive Interaction interventions. I will also consider barriers to providing a naturally warm, touching classroom environment, including fear and notions of age-appropriateness and how these may be overcome so that physical contacts can be rightly viewed as a teaching technique and part of the curriculum (Barnes and Hewett, 2015). These are barely charted seas with very few UK government guidelines to navigate by, but it is possible.

## The social functions of touch

For a moment, let us strip away the trappings of modern society, including digital technology and even clothes. Laid (literally) bare is a highly sociable primate species whose young are the most vulnerable and dependent on care from adults for the longest time of all animal species. From day one, touch is a fundamental part of that care. However sophisticated we might believe our species to be, touch influences how we perceive our interactions. The underpinning for this is the physiological structure and relationship between our nervous system and the largest organ of the human body, the skin (Cascio, Moore and McGlone, 2019). A specialist network of nerve fibres report to the limbic area of the brain, forming our 'social touch system' (Olausson et al., 2010) which responds to nurturing touch and is involved in shaping our emotional responses to situations. It is no accident of nature that our bodies have a sensory touch system that is tuned to the nuances of natural nurturing touches that occur within our species. It is this system that ensures that the giving and receiving of these touches that bind us socially are viewed as a pleasurable experience for both parties and, evolutionarily, enabled our survival.

DOI: 10.4324/9781003170839-11

> Keltner (2010), a prominent researcher in touch, highlights five social functions of touch in humans:
>
> - Provides feeling of reward.
> - Reinforces reciprocity.
> - Signals safety.
> - Soothes.
> - Promotes cooperation.
>
> All are necessary components for a harmonious classroom environment, or, to unpick it even further, all are required for just 'being' with others relationally in the way that is required to participate in Intensive Interaction. I will consider these social functions of touch in terms of Intensive Interaction and classroom practice.

## Provides feeling of reward

Nurturing touch is inherently rewarding. It is linked to the release of the hormone oxytocin, which is associated with the state of calm and connection (Uvnas Moberg, 2003, p. 3). Often learners who require Intensive Interaction are some of the hardest to reach (Barber, 2002) and we use Intensive Interaction precisely because we need to find a way to connect with them. Therefore, nurturing touches that occur naturally within Intensive Interaction help to create states of calm and connection in both parties, in turn supporting the effectiveness of those interactions. A win-win situation.

## Reinforces reciprocity

Studies into primate behaviour show them spending a significant amount of time grooming – more than is beneficial in terms of the removal of lice etc. (Dunbar, 2004). Touches involved in grooming generate cooperative relationships that enable reciprocity. As sophisticated human communicators, we have developed these grooming behaviours into social 'chit-chat' or phatic communications (Hewett, 2012), for example, talking about the weather or last night's *Strictly Come Dancing* TV show. These are conversations that bond us in mutual enjoyment, where the pleasure of the interaction is more important than the sharing of information. Many of our learners are unable to enjoy these phatic communications verbally and the vignette of 'Sadia' considers how touches may be the chit-chat that is not verbally possible.

> Vignette: Sadia is congenitally blind, and her way of greeting a familiar person is to give and receive 'scruffles'. These are touches on the head over the hair involving rubbing with the knuckles when the hand is clenched in a fist or cupping the head in hands and applying gentle pressure. These reciprocal physical touches can last from a couple of seconds up to several minutes and are her way of checking in; 'Hi, how are you? I'm fine. You seem a bit tired actually, but I'm not, I'm excited to be with you'.

Classrooms are complex places and rely on the sharing of space and resources and working to communal goals. This reciprocity achieved through touch may play a part in the human give and take required in our classroom communities.

## Signals safety

Everyone involved in education strives for classrooms to be safe places – it is the driver of the English government's statutory safeguarding guidance; 'Keeping Children Safe in Education' (Department for Education – DfE, 2020). In terms of emotional wellbeing for our students this includes the need for bonds of trust and safety between staff and students (Carpenter and Carpenter, 2020). We are well aware of the instinctive drive to reach out to hold onto someone when we feel anxious or afraid. Whilst I am not suggesting people in education regularly expect students to face real fears or phobias, students might often be removed from their comfort zones by entering an unfamiliar room or participating in a trip to somewhere exciting with potentially overwhelming new sounds, smells, and sensations. In these circumstances, a touchpoint on entering signifies 'trust me, it's ok'. It is an instinctive and effective way in which we signal safety in our classroom communities.

## Soothes

Soothing touch is a naturally nurturing instinct. When someone is distressed and tearful, we might put an arm round them, stroke their arm, or hold their hand. I see these behaviours in staff rooms, corridors, playgrounds, and classrooms in a variety of dyads. With the social distancing measures required because of COVID-19, it has been hard to resist this instinct – if indeed we have been able to. It is worth considering at this point the reciprocal nature of touch and its effects on both the giver and receiver.

> *'In the very act of touching, one is touched in return . . . In touch, the distinction between touching subject and touched object blurs'.*
>
> (Mazis, 1971, p. 323)

At times, classrooms can be stressful places, and the physiological effects of natural nurturing touches can soothe and support those working together.

## Promotes cooperation

Financial interests have resulted in a significant volume of research into celebratory touching, for example high fives and chest bumps, in the National Basket Association (Kraus, Huang and Keltner, 2010). Without delving into the statistics, touches initially appearing to be celebratory when an individual or team is successful in sport have greater impact. So, consider the formal handshakes, jovial high fives or even hugs that form part of educational award ceremonies. These touches are part of our social grooming that bonds us together cooperatively, making our success more likely. Are these touches part of your classroom pedagogy? Alongside words of praise, claps, or cheers are you able to celebrate achievements physically? Sports players in nearly all disciplines do and it generates success.

A further element of social grooming to be aware of is that touch can convey distinct prosocial emotions of anger, fear, disgust, love, gratitude, and envy (Hertenstein et al., 2006). This aspect of touch may be lost on the more sophisticated communicators amongst us who can rapidly judge this at a distance from body language, facial expression, language, and tone of voice. However, for some it may be conveyed in the way that we touch; the way we may remove someone's soiled clothes can indicate anger (Pistorius, 2011), disgust, or love. Which would you say is most appropriate for an individual who is incontinent? Whilst I would not suggest that you should do the tactile equivalent of 'slapping on a smile', this awareness may help you to think through a situation and consider your emotional response(s). I have certainly been at the receiving end of this transfer of emotions from learners who could be considered as having difficulty in expressing themselves. At a time when I was trying to suppress great personal grief, I have had tender, gentle expressions of love in a head resting against me or a hand reaching out to hold my arm. There was no need for words, I felt the emotion expressed in those touches.

Although I have tailored my examples and anecdotes about the physiology and social functions of touch to my experiences in a special needs classroom, they are applicable to classrooms worldwide. There are further reasons why touches may be even more pertinent to learners with autism, SLD, and PMLD. It is therefore worth considering the developmental pertinence of touch and the added importance for people with sensory impairments, which is more prevalent in people with learning difficulties, particularly PMLD, than in the general population (Van Splunder et al., 2006).

## The developmental pertinence of touch

Touch is the first sense to develop at eight weeks gestation and the most strongly developed sense at birth (Denworth, 2015), followed by auditory then visual. As the child develops, the precedence of these senses is reversed (Montagu, 1986). A child at early developmental levels may still be using the tactile modality as their primary sense to engage with and comprehend the world around them, particularly if they have sensory impairment.

Touch is critical to human development, the natural patterns of rocking, swaying, and bouncing provided when an infant is carried by caregivers not only calms a distressed infant (Cascio et al., 2019) but also helps the development of the vestibular and proprioceptive senses needed for vision and balance (Brown, 2018). For a multitude of physical, social, and emotional reasons our learners who we support with Intensive Interaction may not have experienced being touched for 80% of the time they are engaged in interaction, as would be the typically developing infants observed in the seminal research by Stack and Muir (1990).

It is widely recognised that people with SLD or profound and complex needs are likely to experience high levels of touch for the whole of their lives (Dobson et al., 2002, p. 353) – touch to feed, position, keep safe, clean, and maintain good health (Carnaby and Cambridge, 2006); touches that can all be performed safely, efficiently, and hygienically but without addressing an individual's social or developmental touch needs. Furthermore, the use of equipment to maintain good postural care (Public Health England, 2018) means that throughout their lifetimes many people with PMLD will spend a large proportion of their time using equipment that inhibits natural nurturing touches. Melanie Reid, a journalist who became a tetraplegic in 2010 eloquently describes the physical isolation of using a wheelchair:

> '[Y]ou get lots of hugs, but they are brief, fluttery, weedy affairs, your visitor bending over only their arms and shoulders momentarily touching yours. I can no longer give and receive precious spontaneous, full-length hugs'.
>
> (Reid, 2015)

Alongside Carpenter (2010), I would urge anyone to see beyond the physical barriers of positional equipment, to the child as a learner with the same needs for engagement through touch as a non-disabled child. Ironically, it may take additional equipment for you to share relaxed, nurturing touches: mats, sofas, foam rolls, etc. Often, alongside the need for additional equipment, to make these nurturing touches possible, additional timetabling is necessary. Using positional equipment often has to be planned into the school day. Similarly, sitting together in a relaxed way, thus facilitating a comfortable, close environment for Intensive Interaction with natural nurturing touches might have to be scheduled. A mainstream classroom environment with chairs at tables might not be the most conducive positioning to enable Intensive Interactions involving nurturing touches. Do these occur more naturally resting on cushions in a carpeted corner of a classroom, in a swimming pool, or outside? This again needs to be considered and structured into time in school.

# Additional barriers to touching

Looking beyond equipment and timetabling, Hewett (2007, p. 121) discussed ten barriers to touching, which seem as relevant now as they did back then. There is not the space to discuss them all in this chapter, but I would like to consider a few of his points in greater depth:

### Fear of allegations of abuse, other people misconstruing what the member of staff is doing
This is well reported, particularly for male staff members (Culham, 2004; Johnson, 2000, p. 21) and an issue that Piper and Stronach (2008) describe as a 'Moral Panic':

> '[T]he touching of children in professional settings had increasingly stopped being relaxed, or instinctive, or primarily concerned with responding to the needs of the child. It was becoming a self-conscious negative act . . . controlled more by fear than a commitment to caring'.
>
> (ibid., p. X.)

As a practitioner, I feel this has been partly perpetuated through safe-guarding training, which recommends practices such as open doors into classrooms so there is a clear line of sight (ibid, p. 4) and considering the 'snapshot' of how any physical contact would be interpreted by an observer. Along with Hewett (2007, p. 121), I would strongly advise that you document a rationale for touching, both during Intensive Interaction and at all other times. In addition, the use of touch needs to be part of a continuing dialogue within classrooms and with parents, carers, and other professionals. This might be in terms of reflecting on Intensive Interaction practice and student progress but also acknowledging the emotional impact that it can have on us all, particularly in these post-lockdown times when touch has been restricted in all our lives (Barnes, 2020).

## Belief that touching is abuse/belief that it is illegal under the Children's Act

'Keeping Children Safe in Education' is the only statutory document for schools in England that mentions touch and specifically states that staff need to be able to touch:

> 'The department believes that the adoption of a "no contact" policy at a school or college can leave staff unable to fully support and protect their pupils and students. It encourages headteachers, principals, governing bodies and proprietors to adopt sensible policies, which allow and support staff to make appropriate physical contact'.
>
> (DfE, 2020, p. 32)

Whilst this statement has been written from a safe-guarding perspective, particularly considering necessary restraint, it clearly indicates that 'appropriate' touching is expected between staff and students. Elsewhere in the document different types of abuse are defined and explained, clarifying that 'intent' and 'consequences of actions' are abusive, not solely 'touching'.

Without wanting to oversimplify the situation, seeking the learner's consent to be touched is essential to protect both the staff member and pupil. I am under no illusion over the difficulty in achieving this, but it is best practice especially when working with learners who may not anticipate being touched even as part of a regular, established routine, such as wiping their face. The main principles of Intensive Interaction again help us with this process by considering our behaviours of tuning in, simplification, and **pausing** to allow the learner to think and process and **then** indicating their consent, or otherwise.

The all-important dialogue about the use of touch in classrooms should include what consent from a learner 'looks like'. I have seen this successfully documented in communication passports (Millar and Aitken, 2003) with text describing an individual's behaviour that indicates consent, for example, stilling, verbalising, and, importantly, lack of consent, for example, turning away, dropping their head, etc. Where possible the descriptions are paired with photographs to illustrate what can often be subtle behaviours.

Some learners will avoid or react negatively to touch. This can make offering touches above and beyond those necessary to keep them safe and clean feel abusive. Their responses may be due to hypersensitivity of the skin (Ayres and Robbins, 2005), frequently to gentle touches, which may feel painful. Or a learnt response from previous negative experiences associated with touch (McLinden and McCall, 2002). These learners may be described as 'tactile defensive' or perhaps more appropriately 'tactile selective', as it is extremely rare for someone to dislike all touch in all contexts all the time. Families can offer support with identifying the touches that someone does initiate or enjoy, even if they are unconventional.

> Vignette: Jessica struggles with her tactile input, including the sensations of her clothes, particularly seams and labels, and being touched by others. She does enjoy contact with people she is close to and has developed what can be described as the 'no-touch hug' with her family. This involves the recipient remaining still with arms outstretched and not reciprocating as Jessica hugs them. In this way Jessica is able to control the physical sensations she experiences, whilst enabling social touch with the people she loves.

Understanding the learner's comfort zone can allow them an unpressurised, emotionally safe environment to expand this repertoire of touch. The feet of learners with visual impairment may be less sensitive than their hands, so consider a 'feet-first' approach to exploration. Intensive Interaction encourages us to aspire to all learners to have greater access to the social world including touch, so be sensitive and creative.

## Fear of causing sexual arousal with people who are physically mature

This is the 'tip of the iceberg' into the bigger issue of acknowledging the sexuality of people with significant cognitive impairment. Vehmas (2019) identifies that the traditional way to deal with their sexuality is, simply, to ignore it. Respecting our learners involves establishing what is actually occurring without making assumptions. Does an individual become aroused during intimate care when their genitals are being touched, or are they someone who masturbates without the understanding of societal norms? Excessive masturbation in childhood has long been recognised as a symptom of tactile deprivation (McCray, 1978). It is easy to imagine a circumstantially driven spiral where someone who masturbates is provided with more 'personal time' alone, so less time in close contact with others. As a result, when in close contact with others and exposed to the naturally stimulating human pheromones, they become aroused.

> Sexual arousal should not constitute a reason to exclude an individual from joining the social world through Intensive Interaction. It may seem difficult, but open, transparent, and documented conversations are needed with the class team and families to decide on the most appropriate strategies to support an individual in these circumstances. Nind and Hewett (2005) describe this process when reflecting on their work with an individual who masturbated. Be assured that others will be experiencing similar difficulties and seek help from the experiences and expertise of others (e.g. Davies, 1996).

## General crude beliefs in notions of age-appropriateness being more influential than recognition of the need to be more developmentally appropriate

> Vignette: Lewis and Amelia were in different classes but knew each other before starting school. This interaction occurred during a rebound therapy session. At the end of Amelia's turn, Lewis was hoisted onto the trampoline bed next to her ready for his turn. Once detached from the hoist, he rolled over and touched Amelia who smiled and vocalised in response. They shared this enjoyable touchpoint for a few minutes before Lewis moved away from Amelia. She was then hoisted back into her wheelchair, and Lewis's rebound session began. Without that 'crossover' in the session these friends would not have been able to choose to physically interact with each other from the confines of their wheelchairs.

When delivering workshops, I share images of pupils positioned so they can touch, whilst supervised, so they are not at risk of hurting each other. Frequently, a workshop participant states this would not be considered 'appropriate' in their school. (This was pre-COVID-19, so social distancing was not a factor.) When we talk through this difficulty it becomes more complicated and appears to have some kind of age-appropriate connotations that teenagers should not be laid next to each other to play and explore together as infants may be. (Ironically, typically developing teenagers might be doing this, albeit with different motivations, when not observed).

Most practitioners working with secondary school-aged or adults with learning disabilities will describe how notions of age-appropriateness affect what they deliver – from the suitability of the toys, books, stories, and rhymes used in the classroom to the appropriateness of providing comforting hugs and touches when a learner is distressed. However, it is not mentioned in any statutory UK government guidance, and I have never come across a policy in a school that defines age-appropriateness or provides clear guidelines on applying such a definition to the learning environment. The absence of guidance is most probably because the doctrine of age-appropriateness is similar to the Hans Christian Andersen story of the 'Emperor's New Clothes'; people believe that it is an inherent misunderstanding of their view of the situation that is incorrect and follow the actions of a majority rather than questioning the practice. (Perhaps whilst furtively including materials and practices they believe not to be age-appropriate when they are not being observed?).

Nind and Hewett (1996) are two of only a handful of researchers who have discussed age-appropriateness and have documented the historical context. Let us consider, taken to an extreme, that age-appropriateness means people with learning difficulties should only be offered experiences in line with their chronological age.

As we absorb this, consider that many neurotypical adults choose activities like watching Disney films, playing board games, etc. either alone or with other adults. Fundamentally we can be autonomous, able to choose how we spend our leisure time and to whom we disclose this. However, the doctrine of age-appropriateness suggests that someone else has the right to decide which activities and resources someone with learning difficulties should access purely because of their chronological age.

> Furthermore, the existence of notions of age-appropriateness in the UK for around half a century can lead to the uncomfortable feeling that there must be some truth in it. I have had people question how we know that learners do not enjoy more 'adult' pursuits if we deny them the opportunity to experience them. Ignoring notions of age-appropriateness does not mean you limit the experiences of people with learning difficulties but moreover that you do not deny them developmentally pertinent activities. It is in considering factors beyond chronological age and to their communication abilities, level of understanding of the social world, and emotional maturity (Smith, 1998) that we are *truly* respecting an individual.

Let us return to the scenario of the learners positioned where they are able to reach out and touch each other. This chapter has evidenced the need for social touches in all humans, and that is even more pertinent to those at early developmental levels. Positional equipment and lack of mobility precludes them from physically positioning themselves where they can reach each other. Additionally, they may have limited ways to communicate a desire or intention to be close to another. The bonding provided through social touching should not exist solely between staff and students, but opportunities should be created for pupils to form physical bonds with each other.

## Concluding remarks

Intensive Interaction practitioners have so much to consider whilst in the classroom that it is easy to understand how touch could be apportioned only fleeting consideration. Institutional norms and practices could be accepted at face value. I have tried to distil ten years of researching touch into this short chapter. I hope it provokes thought and contemplation of both your own practice and the actions and attitudes of others around you. Whilst the majority of humans have multiple ways to communicate and interact with each other, for those involved in Intensive Interaction interventions, touch may be the most developmentally pertinent channel through which to communicate. Being unable to share safe, nurturing touches may contribute to social isolation. I hope that you will share my belief that touch is not a luxury but a physical foundation that binds us as humans.

# References

Ayres, A. J. and Robbins, J. (2005). *Sensory Integration and the Child: Understanding Hidden Sensory Challenges*. Los Angeles, CA: Western Psychological Services.

Barber, M. (2002). 'The teacher who mistook his pupil for a nuclear incident: Environment influences on people with profound and multiple learning difficulties'. In: P. Farrell and M. Ainscow, eds., *Making Special Education Inclusive: From Research to Practice*. London: Routledge, pp. 183–194.

Barnes, J. (2020). Riding the emotional corona-coaster and its effects on the Touchscape of the classroom. *PMLD Link*, 32(3), Issue 97, pp. 18–20.

Barnes, K. and Hewett, D. (2015). 'Physical contact experiences within the curriculum'. In: P. Lacey et al., eds., *The Routledge Companion to Severe and Profound and Multiple Learning Difficulties*. Cornwall: Routledge, pp. 182–191.

Brown, D. (2018). 'What does multi sensory impairment mean?' In: *Listen to Me: Multi-Sensory Impairment Conference Proceedings*. Manchester, UK.

Carnaby, S. and Cambridge, P. (2006). 'Staff attitudes and perspectives'. In: *Intimate and Personal Care with People with Learning Difficulties*. London: Jessica Kingsley, pp. 18–32.

Carpenter, B. (2010). 'Children with complex learning difficulties and disabilities: Who are they and how do we teach them?' In: *Complex Needs Series*. Great Britain: Specialist Schools and Academies' Trust, pp. 1–6.

Carpenter, B. and Carpenter, M. (2020). *A Recovery Curriculum: Loss and Life for Our Schools and Children and Schools Post Pandemic*. Available at: www.barrycarpentereducation.com [Accessed 8 February 2021].

Cascio, C., Moore, D. and McGlone, F. (2019). Social touch and human development. *Developmental Cognitive Neuroscience*, 35, pp. 5–11.

Culham, A. (2004). Getting in touch with our feminine sides? Men's difficulties and concerns with doing intensive interaction. *British Journal of Special Education*, 31(2), pp. 81–88.

Davies, J. (1996). *Sexuality Education for Children with Visual Impairments: A Parent's Guide*. Available at: www.tsbvi.edu/technology/203-resources/3253-sexuality-education-for-children-with-visual-impairments-a-parents-guide [Accessed 28 December 2020].

Denworth, L. (2015). The social power of touch. *Scientific American Mind*, 26(4), pp. 30–39.

Department for Education, (2020). *Keeping Children Safe in Education*. Available at: www.gov.uk/government/publications/keeping-children-safe-in-education-2 [Accessed 5 October 2020].

Dobson, S., Upadhyaya, S., Conyers, I. and Raghavan, R. (2002). Touch in the care of people with profound and complex needs: A review of the literature. *Journal of Intellectual Disabilities*, 6(4), pp. 352–362.

Dunbar, P. R. (2004). *Grooming, Gossip and the Evolution of Language*. New Edition. London and Boston: Faber & Faber.

Hertenstein, M., Keltner, D., App, B., Bulleit, B. A. and Jaskolka, A. R. (2006). Touch communicates distinct emotions. *Emotion*, 6(3), pp. 528–533.

Hewett, D. (2007). Do touch – Physical contact and those who have severe, profound and multiple learning difficulties. *Support for Learning*, 22(3), pp. 116–123.

Hewett, D. (2012). 'Blind frogs: The nature of human communication and Intensive Interaction'. In: D. Hewett, ed., *Intensive Interaction: Theoretical Perspectives*. London: Sage Publications, pp. 4–21.

Johnson, R. (2000). '"No touch" as moral panic'. In: *Hands Off! The Disappearance of Touch in the Care of Children*. New York: Peter Lang, pp. 17–34.

Keltner, D. (2010). *Hands on Research: The Science of Touch*. Available at: https://greatergood.berkeley.edu/article/item/hands_on_research [Accessed 3 October 2020].

Kraus, M., Huang, C. and Keltner, D. (2010). Tactile communication, cooperation and performance: An ethological study of the NBE. *Emotion*, 10, pp. 745–749.

Mazis, G. (1971). Touch and vision: Rethinking with Merleau-Ponty and Sartre on the caress. *Psychology Today*, 23, pp. 231–328.

McCray, G. (1978). Excessive masturbation of childhood: A symptom of tactile deprivation? *Pediatrics*, 62(3), pp. 277–279.

McLinden, M. and McCall, S. (2002). *Learning Through Touch: Supporting Children with Visual Impairment and Additional Difficulties*. 1st ed. Abingdon: David Fulton Publishers.

Millar, S. and Aitken, S. (2003). *Personal Communication Passports: Guidelines for Good Practice*. Edinburgh: University of Edinburgh CALL Centre.

Montagu, A. (1986). *Touching: The Human Significance of the Skin*. New York: Harper.

Nind, M. and Hewett, D. (1996). 'When age-appropriateness isn't appropriate'. In: J. Coupe-O'Kane and J. Goldbart, eds., *Whose Choice? Contentious Issues for Those Working with People with Learning Difficulties*. Abingdon: David Fulton Publishers, pp. 48–57.

Nind, M. and Hewett, D. (2005). *Access to Communication: Developing the Basics of Communication for People Who Have Severe Learning Disabilities Through Intensive Interaction*. 2nd ed. Abingdon: David Fulton Publishers.

Olausson, H., Wessberg, J., Morrison, I., McGlone, F. and Valbo, A. (2010). The neurophysiology of unmyelinated tactile afferents. *Neuroscience and Biobehavioral Reviews*, 34, pp. 185–191.

Piper, H. and Stronach, I. (2008). *Don't Touch! The Educational Story of Panic*. Oxon: Routledge.

Pistorius, M. (2011). *Ghost Boy: My Escape from a Life Locked Inside My Own Body*. London: Simon & Schuster.

Public Health England. (2018). *Postural Care and People with Learning Disabilities; Guidance*. Available at: www.gov.uk/government/publications/postural-care-services-making-reasonable-adjustments/postural-care-and-people-with-learning-disabilities [Accessed 22 February 2021].

Reid, M. (2015). Spinal column. *The Times Magazine*, 3 January, p. 11.

Smith, C. (1998). 'Jamie's story: Intensive Interaction in a college of further education'. In: D. Hewett and M. Nind, eds., *Interaction in Action: Reflections on the Use of Intensive Interaction*. London: David Fulton Publishers, pp. 46–63.

Stack, D. and Muir, D. (1990). Tactile stimulation as a component of social interchange: New interpretations for the still-face effect. *British Journal of Developmental Psychology*, 8, pp. 131–145.

Uvnas Moberg, K. (2003). *The Oxytocin Factor*. Boston, MA: De Capo.

Van Splunder, J., Stilma, J. S., Bernsen, R. M. D. and Evenhuis, H. M. (2006). Prevalence of visual impairment in adults with intellectual disabilities in the Netherlands: Cross-sectional study. *Eye*, 20(9), pp. 1004–1010.

Vehmas, S. (2019). Persons with profound intellectual disability and their right to sex. *Disability and Society*, 34(4), pp. 519–539.

# 12. Management issues
## Ensuring a school is Intensive Interaction friendly

*Anne Adams*

## Introduction

As an Intensive Interaction practitioner since the early 1990s, teaching in special schools in London and in Shropshire, initially my focus was on making a difference to individual children in my class and then across a whole class group. As my career developed to include cross-school leadership responsibilities, the imperative to make a difference to the wider school community brought with it emerging opportunities and challenges. These came particularly into focus in 2010 upon becoming the Head Teacher of an independent special school for children and young people aged 8–19. All the students had autism, learning disabilities, and complex needs, including trauma and the potential to exhibit extreme levels of challenge, and all had been excluded from their previous schools as a result. This chapter will look at the opportunities this new role provided but also acknowledges the challenges.

## Recognising priorities: why should school leaders prioritise Intensive Interaction?

### Values driven

> As a school leader I believe we have a moral imperative to reflect upon and make a conscious decision about how we choose to lead. For me, the focus has been on promoting and supporting an emotionally and physically healthy organisation that supports a high-quality learning community for all (students and staff alike). I believe this needs to be founded on high-quality empathic relationships and communication and interaction, where all stakeholders have respect for themselves and each other. All humans have an innate need to feel safe, to connect, and to be social, regardless of their disability or experience.

Most, if not all, leadership and management texts and training emphasise the importance of leaders effectively communicating and getting teams to buy into the organisation's vision and values in order to develop a strong and supportive culture. Although this may sound a bit clichéd and familiar, my honestly

DOI: 10.4324/9781003170839-12

held belief and experience holds this as true. For me, when talking about values, it is not about staff being able to quote the school vision and values 'straplines' or flashy signage and displays. Outlining a vision should give a clear direction and destination which everyone in your school team can move towards, but most importantly, everyone needs to be clear about how those values translate into their behaviours.

Anyone who knows me will be very aware that I am not a football fan, so may well be more than surprised that I will here reference Pep Guardiola (Hughes, 2018) who, as manager of the highly successful FC Barcelona said, 'A team's culture is about the conduct and behaviour of everyone involved, it's working together towards shared objectives and, as such, is an immediately identifiable part of the group's identity'. This quote is shared by Professor Damian Hughes (2018), who analyses the success of FC Barcelona under Guardiola's management and in doing so identifies four factors in creating a 'commitment culture' to make your vision become a reality: **imagination** (where you sell your vision of what you are trying to achieve and why), **illustration** (where you show people how you are going to do it), **participation** (allowing and encouraging people to participate in the plan), and **integration** (embedding the vision as reality). Reflecting on these four areas has enabled me to better understand why my initial efforts to embed Intensive Interaction were not as successful as I had hoped and how we got to where we are today.

> If we accept that values are at the heart of a school's organisation and leadership, then, as a school leader, it is imperative you support staff in truly understanding how your school values translate into expected behaviours. This needs to be done in a myriad of ways, through continuous professional development, through articulating how those values inform your own decision-making, but most importantly by living those values yourself – modelling those value-driven behaviours in your own daily practice in your interactions with children, families, staff, and visitors.

As an independent school, my current setting is part of a larger group, and during my 11 years (so far) with them our group values have changed in wording, although not in their essential content, a few times. However, like most schools (including, I am sure, your own), they have always included words that inspire aspiration, celebrate individuality, and support inclusivity. In our setting (which, as well as the school, includes an on-site children's home) we pride ourselves on our approach being both autism and trauma informed. To support us in this, we follow the National Autistic Society's SPELL (2021 – Structure, Positive, Empathy, Low-arousal, Links) approach combined with trauma and mental-health–informed best practice (Trauma Informed Schools UK – TISUK, 2021), which incorporates PACE principles (Playful, Acceptance, Caring and Empathic – Hughes, Golding and Hudson, 2019). These come with a shared value base that includes the importance of honesty, respect, and empathy. These values are made explicit as part of every staff member's induction training programme and throughout their continuous professional development. We believe it is important for staff to understand not just what the words in the value statement mean but to take ownership of how that influences their working practice and them as a person (see also Appendix 3).

> For those of you who are already practitioners of Intensive Interaction, I am sure you can see how focusing on the Fundamentals of Communication 1 and 2 – emotional and psychological developments (Hewett, 2018) – fully embodies these values. You will also be able to accurately describe how the behaviours of an Intensive Interaction practitioner, who is 'tuning in', going with the tempo of the young person, being responsive and joining in, allowing processing time, in a bubble of mutual enjoyment – perfectly illustrates those values in action.

As a school leader, to share your vision of an Intensive Interaction community, you will need to be able to articulate what you want to achieve and why. Being able to articulate how the practice of Intensive Interaction gives staff the behaviours known to promote communication and interaction skills and emotional development as the fundamentals of holistic development and overall well-being makes this clearly understandable for all stakeholders. My experience has been that a staff team aware of what behaviours they need as an Intensive Interaction practitioner, can match those they need to be an emotionally available adult, not just for the young people they are supporting but also for those young people's family members and for their colleagues.

# Accountability

The children and young people who attend our school all have Education, Health and Care Plans (EHC Plans) that specify areas of need in communication and interaction, and social, emotional, and mental health as priorities. Therefore, it should hopefully be obvious to all that those must also be our whole-school priorities. Fortunately, that is probably more now than ever supported in the legislative formats of the Children and Families Act (The Stationery Office, 2014): Section 19, which leads us to the 'Special Educational Needs and Disability Code of Practice: 0 to 25 years' (Department for Education – DfE, 2015) – most commonly referred to as the SEND Code of Practice, and in the Ofsted Framework (2019a). (I'm sorry, but as a Head Teacher you did not really expect me not to mention Ofsted!)

> ## The SEND Code of Practice – key principles
> 
> The SEND Code of Practice has some key principles underpinning it which are very helpful to us. It categorically states that local authorities:
> 
> 'must have regard to:
> 
> - the views, wishes and feelings of the child or young person, and the child's parents.

> - the importance of the child or young person, and the child's parents, participating as fully as possible in decisions, and being provided with the information and support necessary to enable participation in those decisions.
> - the need to support the child or young person, and the child's parents, in order to facilitate the development of the child or young person and to help them achieve the best possible educational and other outcomes, preparing them effectively for adulthood'. (p. 20)

It goes on to say that these principles are designed to support, among other things, 'High quality provision' and 'a focus on inclusive practice and removing barriers to learning'. They describe that high-quality provision should 'promote positive outcomes in the wider areas of personal and social development, and ensure that the approaches used are based on the best possible evidence and are having the required impact on progress' (DfE, 2015, p. 19).

Once again, for those of you who are already Intensive Interaction practitioners, it is clear to see how the aims, principles, and progress outcomes of Intensive Interaction fill this brief. For anyone reading this chapter who feels they need to know more, we are fortunate to have a wealth of published literature to which you can turn, with *The Intensive Interaction Handbook* (Hewett, 2018) and *Integrating Intensive Interaction* (Mourière and McKim, 2018) being just two very easily accessible examples. Additionally, the Intensive Interaction Institute website offers access to a wealth of video examples, information on training, articles, and further support (intensiveinteraction.org, 2021).

On a practical level, the SEND Code of Practice means that we as a school must ensure our 'SEN Information Report' is published, including the use of Intensive Interaction in details of our approach to teaching children and young people with SEND; in details of accessibility to our broad and balanced curriculum; in the expertise and training of our staff; and in our support for improving emotional and social development. Our children and young people's EHC Plans ensure the educational provision meets their special educational needs to secure the best possible outcomes for them across education, health, and social care and, as they get older, prepare them for adulthood. Ensuring a child or young person's Section E: 'Outcomes' includes a focus on communication and interaction priorities, with Section F: 'Provision' including Intensive Interaction as a strategy is helpful and supportive to all informal and statutory review processes (see Chapter 13). The SEND Code of Practice itself defines an outcome as 'the benefit or difference made to an individual as a result of an intervention' (p. 47).

When a child or young person joins our school without this within their EHC Plans, the statutory review process can be used, as detailed in the SEND Code of Practice, to 'review the special educational provision made for the child or young person to ensure it is being effective in ensuring access to teaching and learning and good progress" and "where appropriate, agree new outcomes' (p. 195). Schools are in a powerful position to impact upon the content of the EHC Plans, in liaison with the child or young person and their family. The SEND Code of Practice (p. 197) states that:

> Reviews are generally most effective when led by the educational institution. They know the child or young person best, will have the closest contact with them and their family and will have the clearest information about progress and next steps. Reviews led by the educational institution will engender the greatest confidence amongst the child, young person and their family.

If your vision and values are clearly articulated, this should reduce the challenge to any input into initial or reviewed EHC Plans because all stakeholders (the child and their family, the local authority, etc.) should hopefully then be clear about what a placement at your school looks like and the provision that you offer (see Chapter 13 for more information and tips for writing an EHC Plan which meets individual needs).

## Ofsted

As I am sure all readers are aware, The Ofsted Inspection Handbook (Non-association independent school inspection handbook, 2019b, p. 34) details that 'Inspectors will assess a school's entire provision, including any specialist provision offered, when reaching judgements in the following areas: overall effectiveness; behaviour and attitudes; personal development; and leadership and management'.

---

### The introduction of 'curriculum intent, implementation, and impact' in the new Ofsted framework has encouraged us all to

- Re-focus on what end points our school curriculum is building towards and the foundations and sequence of knowledge and skills towards those agreed end points.
- Ensure that leaders and all members of the school community are secure in their understanding of FoCs 1 and 2 as being crucial to all future learning and to emotional well-being in order to engage and progress holistically.
- Clearly detail that in our curriculum 'intent'.
- Talk about it openly and frequently so staff at all levels are able to articulate this clearly to all stakeholders (including an Ofsted inspector).
- Evaluate how the curriculum is 'implemented' at classroom level, with staff exhibiting high-quality interactions as part of their everyday behaviours.
- And to be able to articulate why we are working in that way, clearly evidencing staff expert knowledge.

As inspectors focus on what children and young people have learned, with 'all learning building towards an end point', I am confident that your impact will be clear to see. With the embedded use of Intensive Interaction effectively supporting progress due to its focus on communication, interaction, and emotional well-being, this will be the case regardless of the progress and achievement measure your school uses.

Ofsted 'outstanding' criteria, lifted from across the handbook (2019b), includes such words/phrases as 'pupils with SEND achieve exceptionally well', 'high levels of respect for others', 'difference is valued and nurtured', 'consistently positive attitudes', 'goes beyond the expected', 'rich set of experiences', 'opportunities . . . to develop their talents and interests are of exceptional quality', 'developing pupils' character is exemplary', 'highly effective and meaningful engagement . . . with staff'. For me, and I hope for all of you with some knowledge of Intensive Interaction, it is so easy to see how Intensive Interaction embedded across a school supports such statements.

As I write this, our school was last inspected in 2018 while awaiting the new framework but with inspectors very aware of what was coming. I am pleased to say that having Intensive Interaction as part of the foundation of all we do led to such comments in our report as 'well-being is at the heart of everything that staff do', 'pupils develop trusting relationships with staff, all staff share a passion for pupils' well-being and display this in their interactions with the pupils', 'staff are exceptionally caring and responsive to pupils' needs', and that leaders had 'created a school where staff show genuine care for pupils' wide ranging needs'. Hopefully that will give those of you who are leaders the confidence that Ofsted inspectors will 'get it', and that my own perception that a relationship-based approach, incorporating Intensive Interaction at its heart, has been successful in creating the school culture for which I hoped.

### Our children, young people, and their families

Ultimately, of course, it is to our children, young people, and their families to whom we are most accountable. We may be regularly audited by Ofsted, Autism Accreditation, local authorities in the form of virtual school audits, independent reviewing officers, social workers, etc. All those systems quite rightly include pupil voice and seek the views of families. But on a daily, minute-by-minute basis we must be child-centred in every decision we make. This encompasses how we respond to a young person's connection-seeking at that moment in time (including ensuring we are always available and alert for those moments), how we have planned to structure their day (the resources put in place at individual, class, and whole-school level) and future-strategy decisions as part of school improvement planning.

> As staff, no matter what our role, we need to understand how power and privilege dynamics can either enable us to create a positive environment for each child and young person or can undermine individual needs. Each child needs to have their needs understood, listened to, and empowered to

> have influence over their daily life. This is something that Intensive Interaction can help us to ensure is in place. However, as leaders, we need to ensure the staff feel that the same is in place for them, to fully empower them to do the same for those children and young people they are supporting. A staff member is not going to be an effective Intensive Interaction practitioner and be fully available to a child and young person if they do not feel valued and listened to themselves.

## So how can this be achieved?

### Sustainability: introduction, maintenance, and guarding against practice decay

So, as a leader you have shared your **imagination** and your **intent** – you have clearly articulated your vision and values for all stakeholders of how you want your school to be, with Intensive Interaction embedded as part of your culture, and why – in order to promote best outcomes for every child and young person. The next step is to **illustrate** how. What will your **implementation** look like in practice? For this, you will of course need to turn to your school policies so you can spell it out clearly. This may include Intensive Interaction as a strategy in your teaching and learning policy, your communication and interaction policy, and/or others. It will definitely require investment in staff training and continuing professional development (CPD). As previously mentioned, we use staff induction to begin that embedding of values and behaviours. This includes a brief introduction to Intensive Interaction for all staff – no matter their role, including administration and facilities staff. For education staff, Intensive Interaction training is then ongoing – as stand-alone training and referenced within other training packages, such as positive behaviour support and trauma-informed practice.

However, outside of timetabled training and CPD, the most powerful illustration has to be 'in the moment' modelling and coaching of best practice. This can include that which is planned as part of staff professional development, but often the most powerful are those unplanned-for 'golden moments', for example, when a child or young person unexpectedly joins you in your office and you stop typing up your Report for Governors and choose to give them your undivided attention for as long as they request it instead. Or when you divert from a planned learning walk because a child takes you by the hand to the swings instead. Or when you hear a young person really sad or distressed and you leave your office to 'get in the hole' with them and empathise with how they are feeling – even if that is just with your body language and no words. You being flexible with your own timetable/plans also helps to give your staff permission to do the same, putting the needs of the child in the moment before what their schedule or timetable may say. Remember, what you do is always going to be more powerful than what you say. However, **participation** for sustainability is key – it can't all be on you as an individual, no matter what role you have in the school.

So, this is the reality check. As previously stated, I am a long-term practitioner and huge advocate of Intensive Interaction. In my previous setting (a 300+ place generic special school), I was incredibly fortunate to be funded by the school to complete my Intensive Interaction Coordinator's course – which not only strengthened and deepened my own knowledge, understanding, and practice but upskilled me in training others. I had clearly been successful in enabling the leadership of that school to recognise the benefits because when I left they invested in two more staff completing the Coordinator's course to help to continue to develop and sustain Intensive Interaction across the school. So as a new Head teacher of a very small school back in 2010, I thought it would be a cinch to get Intensive Interaction introduced and embedded across the school. In my first available training day, I gave all staff a full one-day training. Staff were positive and keen to implement Intensive Interaction, some even volunteered to be part of a pilot precursor to something similar to what is now the Intensive Interaction Institute 'Good Practice' course – with me taking them through it.

Those of you who are experienced leaders can probably predict what happened next and consider me very naïve. As a new Head Teacher of that small but rapidly growing school (which had also been without a Head Teacher for a while), there were quite a few other demands upon my time and energy. No one else at that time had the knowledge or experience of Intensive Interaction to fully support its embedding, and although some amazing practice continued in pockets, it was far from being consistent across the school. I was aware of this and saddened by it, but I had to acknowledge that I needed support for myself in order to re-energise the whole school. With perfect timing, the Intensive Interaction Institute began to offer its Coordinator refresher course. Taking two days out of school and allocating a chunk of our school training budget to my own CPD was not an easy decision, but with the encouragement of my School Improvement Partner, I did – and both I, and the school, have not looked back since!

Key to this was the realisation I had to 'let go'. Intensive Interaction could remain a passion for me, but I had to be prepared to share its leadership and empower the participation of others. I have done this through joint working with my talented Deputy Head, who comes to Intensive Interaction via a positive behaviour support and emotional well-being expertise angle, and a superb Speech and Language Therapist, who brings autism and trauma-informed specialisms to her total communication approach. In addition, we now have a whole team of key staff members (from education, care, and clinical) completing the Intensive Interaction Institute 'Good Practice' course, part of which is sharing and cascading their learning to others. Key for me has been getting to the point where I get just as much of a thrill from seeing amazing practice of a staff member interacting with a child or young person as from being in that bubble myself.

> This means appreciating the need to focus time, energy, and resources into the support of others to lead, train, and model best practice. It is no good me expecting them to achieve where I failed in supporting the embedding of Intensive Interaction across the school, if I do not give them the support that I lacked – in terms of CPD, time, and emotional support as needed. Most importantly, they need to feel valued and empowered.

## Intensive Interaction documentation

Some mention has been made of key documentation already in this chapter, and it is crucial for supporting your **integration** or embedding of practice as part of your values and culture, as well as clarifying what your **impact** measures are. For me, the simplest thing is to remember that if it isn't written down it doesn't happen, or, if you prefer, does your documentation 'say it like it is'? This is about 'making your vision a reality and ensuring your way of doing things is embedded' (Hughes, 2018). At our school we talk about having a 'golden thread'. For us, what that means is the following: ensuring that our approach, with Intensive Interaction at the heart of that, starts by being stated openly in our Prospectus and in our SEN Information Report.

---

### Embedding your vision within school documentation

'We use the principles of the National Autistic Society (NAS) SPELL and a Trauma Informed approach in order to maximise access to the whole curriculum as well as being trauma and mental health informed.

- **S**tructure: including how we organise the environment, use of personal schedules and systematic strategies to work. So creating a highly structured and predictable environment.
- **P**ositive: approaches and expectations through sensitive but persistent intervention based upon thorough individual assessment, including Intensive Interaction and play-based approaches. Supporting children to develop the capacity for self-regulation; a "no matter what" approach.
- **E**mpathy: based upon respect for personal experience to inform what motivates and what may frighten, preoccupy or distress each individual. Relationships, connection and belonging are central to our school ethos; one size does not fit all and we are adaptive to the needs and requirements of each child.
- **L**ow arousal: based upon individual sensory profiles and the use of PRICE (Protecting Rights In a Caring Environment) for the positive management of potentially challenging behaviour. Creating an environment of psychological and physical safety is fundamental; behaviour is viewed as communication and with curiosity.
- **L**inks: through a thematic approach to the curriculum and a multi-disciplinary team-work approach across the service and with families/significant others. Whole school ethos that has a common language, consistency and understanding, based upon neuro-science'.

---

We then reinforce that through various policies, including the communication policy, which includes Intensive Interaction as a key way of working. It is also included in our autism policy:

'At Options Higford we ensure we support children and young people who have difficulty with social understanding in the following ways:

*Intensive Interaction is used to give children and young people enjoyable and relaxing experiences of interaction that they have some control over and to support the development of the fundamentals of communication'.*

*. . . and so on.*

Then to continue that 'golden thread', you will find Intensive Interaction referred to in EHC Plans:

*Provide a total communication environment that includes the use of Intensive Interaction by readily available staff throughout the day, with regular and frequent opportunities and reasons to communicate throughout each day.*

Which then gets carried through to their Individual Education Plan.

---

# Example of an individual positive behaviour support plan

## Support (name) to use positive behaviour, engagement, and Intensive Interaction

- Each time (name) approaches you use positive and fun interaction to motivate engagement. Reduce interaction when (name) is using behaviours that challenge.
- Respond promptly when (name) initiates appropriate fun interaction or responds to instruction but provide good role modelling when necessary to help develop their understanding of appropriate social skills and interaction.

### Problem solving

- Support (name) to identify problems and solve them rather than fixing the problem for them, for example, 'uh-oh, stuck'. Let (name) 'do the doing' with 'hand over hand' support, rather than fixing it for them, but simplify the problem if their arousal level increases.

### Communication

- Use the Intensive Interaction approach to encourage shared attention and engagement.
- Use a total communication approach (multiple modes of communication).

> **Regulation**
> - If (name) appears anxious, with simple single words, encourage him to indicate what the problem is on his communication book.
> - Help (name) to find ways of reducing his anxiety to aid his self-regulation skills by guiding him to a soothing activity and remaining connected with him, for example, directing him to a quiet area; listening to music.

And, of course, within Individual Communication Plans – for example:

> ## General advice and guidance
> - *Use the Intensive Interaction approach to encourage shared attention and engagement.*
> - *Give (name) lots of processing time, especially in busy, noisy environments.*
> - *Use a Total Communication approach (use of multiple modes of communication to give (name)) the best possible chance of understanding.*
> - *Only use single words and support the use of these with exaggerated gestures (e.g. nodding head for 'yes'), early Makaton signs (e.g. more, gone, finished) and visual contextual cues (objects, photos, and clear symbols of reference).*
> - *The vocabulary of words used should only relate to the person, thing, activity, and place that is the focus at any given time.*
> - *'Wrap' language around all activity in the form of a commentary at the single word level.*
> - *Support spoken language with high use of affect (gesture, nonverbal communication, and the voice).*
> - *Provide lots of opportunity for shared attention, engagement, and interaction in routine and play-based activities.*
> - *Use affect (nonverbal communication, gesture, and the voice) in a playful way to encourage shared attention/engagement in a nurturing way to support regulation and gently but firmly when setting boundaries.*

This is of course then carried through and referenced within any planning and progress documentation, including Annual EHC Plan Review reports and Annual Reports to Parents, for example:

*(Name) has taken part in many activities that have supported his communication; however, the biggest changes have come within himself. (Name) seems to be more willing to let others in and has accepted support from the multi-disciplinary team to help him communicate his wants and needs,*

*pain and his sensory needs. Staff have been focusing on using Intensive Interaction with (name); this has supported and affected how we, as a team, communicate with him when he is in distress. We have been able to reduce the amount of times we have used his helmet and given him the opportunity to ask for a head massage and put pressure on the points where he needs the sensory input.*

## Concluding remarks

I am not sure 'concluding' is really the right word here – as there is always more to be done. Embedding Intensive Interaction, as with any aspect of best practice, is always going to be an ongoing journey with a destination that is never quite reached because you add to or amend your vision through continual reflective practice.

However, in a nutshell I would probably like to say, if you are the person driving forward Intensive Interaction in your school, always ensure you are kind to yourself and build in opportunities for those high-quality interactions that you need to meet your own communication and emotional needs as part of your working practice – don't try and be the hero who does it all by themselves. Always lead by example, but share your vision: empower and include others, rather than seeing it as a personal mission. Be realistic and not disheartened by anything that may get in the way of achieving your aims immediately – just keep hold of your enthusiasm and integrity – it may take longer or be via a less direct route to get to where you want to be, but use that as an opportunity for reflective practice rather than a barrier to progress.

And what are our next steps? Definitely continuing our promotion of others to lead, inspire, and innovate. More work with parents and carers (a challenge when many of our families live a considerable distance from the school) and embedding Intensive Interaction across our onsite children's home as well as within the school. Exciting times!

## References

Department for Education, (2015). *Special Educational Needs and Disability Code of Practice: 0 to 25 Years*. Available at: https://assets.publishing.service.gov.uk/government/uploads/system/uploads/attachment_data/file/398815/SEND_Code_of_Practice_January_2015.pdf [Accessed 21 January 2021].

Hewett, D. (ed.) (2018). *The Intensive Interaction Handbook*. 2nd ed. London: Sage Publications.

Hughes, D. (2018). *The Barcelona Way: How to Create a High-Performance Culture*. London: Macmillan.

Hughes, D. A., Golding, K. S. and Hudson, J. (2019). *Healing Relational Trauma with Attachment-Focused Interventions*. New York: W. W. Norton and Company.

Mourière, A. and McKim, J. (eds.) (2018). *Integrating Intensive Interaction*. London and New York: Routledge.

National Autistic Society, (2021). *Strategies and Interventions – SPELL*. Available at: www.autism.org.uk/advice-and-guidance/topics/strategies-and-interventions/strategies-and-interventions/spell [Accessed 21 February 2021].

Office for Standards in Education (Ofsted), (2019a). *The Education Inspection Framework*. Available at: https://assets.publishing.service.gov.uk/government/uploads/system/uploads/attachment_data/file/801429/Education_inspection_framework.pdf [Accessed 21 February 2021].

Office for Standards in Education (Ofsted), (2019b). *Non-Association Independent School Inspection Handbook – Handbook for Inspecting Non-Association Independent Schools in England Under Section 109(1) and (2) of the Education and Skills Act 2008*. Available at: https://assets.publishing.service.gov.uk/government/uploads/system/uploads/attachment_data/file/841974/Non-association_independent_school_handbook.pdf [Accessed 25 February 2021].

The Intensive Interaction Institute. Available at: www.intensiveinteraction.org [Accessed 21 February 2021].

The Stationery Office, (2014). *Children and Families Act*. Available at: www.legislation.gov.uk/ukpga/2014/6/pdfs/ukpga_20140006_en.pdf [Accessed 21 February 2021].

Trauma Informed Schools UK (TISUK) (2021). Available at: www.traumainformedschools.co.uk [Accessed 21 February 2021].

# 13. Ensuring access to Intensive Interaction through Education, Health and Care Plans

*Lucy Hankin*

## Introduction

Over the recent years, there have been several educational reforms which have created the capacity for change within special education settings. The SEND Code of Practice (Department for Education and Department of Health – DfE & DoH, 2015), the move to Education, Health and Care (EHC) Plans, and the Rochford Review (Standards and Testing Agency, 2016) have led many schools to review the way in which they plan for their pupils' education.

> Many schools are now placing even greater emphasis on the role of EHC Plans in shaping the curriculum for their pupils. EHC Plans, as legal documents, must be followed, and the information within must reflect an individual's unique development and learning needs.

As an Intensive Interaction Coordinator within a special school for pupils with autism, my role is to embed Intensive Interaction into as much of school life as possible, ensuring good quality provision is available to all those who need it. It became increasingly clear that EHC Plans should document the need for Intensive Interaction, outlining the associated aims and outcomes. This much was obvious, the intricacies of how to make sure this would happen, and in the right way, was more of a challenge. Not only did I need to explore the 'right way' to document the need for Intensive Interaction, but also, importantly, I needed to establish a plan to embed this as common practice within my setting.

## EHC Plans – the importance of 'getting it right'

EHC Plans are governed by the guidance given in the SEND Code of Practice (2015). This sets out what information should be included and offers guidelines for doing so. We must adhere to these guidelines and at the same time ensure we maintain the principles of Intensive Interaction.

DOI: 10.4324/9781003170839-13

> Intensive Interaction is clearly defined as a process-central approach (Hewett et al., 2012), and this is exactly what supports its associated learning outcomes: the Fundamentals of Communication (FoCs – Nind and Hewett, 2001 – see Chapter 3). As such, these learning outcomes will only happen if the integrity of the approach and its principles are maintained: a process-central approach, led by the pupil, at the right pace, with a sensitively tuned-in and responsive learning partner. It is crucial that these principles are reflected in the documentation to safeguard the development of the FoCs. If, by attempting to 'fit' Intensive Interaction into a document, we change any of the key principles of the approach, it is simply no longer Intensive Interaction, and this could negatively impact upon the development of the FoCs.

Given the increasingly important role EHC Plans have in shaping the curriculum, there is even greater responsibility to make sure that the information included is accurate and representative of the way in which Intensive Interaction should happen within the classroom. The information included within EHC Plans will have a direct impact on classroom practices and curriculum planning. If the information included is too brief or misinformed, there is a real danger of classroom practice suffering, to the detriment of the learners.

A well-written EHC Plan will ensure that the individual gets the support they need throughout their education. As a legal document, if we get it right from the start, it gives parents and educators the power to ensure that Intensive Interaction is included within the individual's provision as a statutory requirement from Early Years to Primary, Secondary, Post-16, and even onto Adult Services.

## Establishing best practice documentation of Intensive Interaction – how to 'get it right'

I began to investigate the degree to which Intensive Interaction was already included within EHC Plans in my setting. I found that it was already referenced in several of them, but sometimes this reference was brief, limited to one section only, and often did not reference the detailed learning outcomes of the FoCs. Although it is a positive step forward for Intensive Interaction to be included in any way, I started to explore what the best way would be to fully acknowledge the breadth of its learning and impact. In doing so, I tried to establish what well-written EHC Plans had in common, taking account of the SEND Code of Practice guidance as well as examples from established practitioners. It became clear that well-written EHC Plans follow a 'golden thread', linking aspirations, needs, outcomes, and provision (Delivering Better Outcomes Together Consortium, n.d.). Therefore, references to both the FoCs and Intensive Interaction should be woven throughout the EHC Plan, rather than being included in isolation.

## Writing Intensive Interaction within the EHC Plan

The essential sections to consider are:

- Section A: views, interests, and aspirations – Includes information about how pupils engage in Intensive Interaction on a daily basis.
- Section B: special educational needs – Considers an individual's strengths and needs relating to social interaction, including their development of the FoCs 1 and 2.
- Section E: outcomes – Outlines the development of the FoCs as a priority.
- Section F: provision – Identifies Intensive Interaction as the appropriate provision to support the development of the FoCs.

## Section A: views, interests, and aspirations

Section A sets out to establish the views, interests, and aspirations of the individual (DfE & DoH, 2015, p. 161). Often, One Page Profiles are used to support this, including key information about things that are important to the child and what makes them happy, likes/dislikes, and approaches to supporting them. They should be written by people who know the individual well (parents, staff, and other professionals involved with them).

If possible, Intensive Interaction should be included here and referred to by name, describing the way in which it is used with the individual, for example:

*I enjoy building relationships with new staff through Intensive Interaction;*

*I am starting to notice the other adults and children in class. Please help me learn to develop my social interaction skills by using Intensive Interaction with me.*

Intensive Interaction will often be a key approach to supporting individuals: including its techniques can be useful here (tuning-in, pausing, not doing too much, being responsive, mutual enjoyment):

*If I am feeling distressed, Intensive Interaction can help me connect with those around me: help me by stepping back, getting lower down (if safe), staying tuned-in and remembering pauses may be longer than usual as I process everything going on around me.*

This can also be a good opportunity to write down specific ways in which you have noticed that individuals seek and initiate interactions, particularly if they are unique to the individual and may otherwise be dismissed.

*Sometimes I will reach out to staff with one of my toys in hand, this usually means I am seeking interaction and am ready to engage with Intensive Interaction.*

## Section B: special educational needs

Initially, this is written using contributions from an assessment team, but it can be reviewed and amended at each Annual Review. If a child joins your class and you feel they would benefit from Intensive Interaction, use this opportunity to include it in this section, considering their strengths and needs around the FoCs.

It is possible to include Intensive Interaction in all the areas of need referenced within the EHC Plan as the FoCs underpin all areas of learning.

See the EHC Plan example in Table 13.1.

## Sections E and F: outcomes and provision

There is an important distinction to make between outcomes and provision. Outcomes are defined by the SEND Code of Practice as 'the benefit or difference made to an individual as a result of an intervention' (DfE & DoH, 2015, p. 163).

Provision is the support or intervention required to support the special educational needs identified in Section B. It must be 'specified for each and every need' and should show how it will 'support achievement of the outcomes' (ibid., 166.), showing a clear link between needs, provision, and outcomes.

Where Section B identifies special educational needs relating to the FoCs 1 and 2, the provision to support this is Intensive Interaction; outcomes should focus on the development of the FoCs 1 and 2.

# Writing Intensive Interaction outcomes for the EHC Plan – Section E

The SEND Code of Practice suggests outcomes should be SMART: specific, measurable, achievable, realistic, and time-bound (DfE & DoH, 2015, p. 163). It also acknowledges that outcomes may include developing 'positive social relationships . . . emotional resilience and stability' (ibid., 162). However, social communication and interaction learning is not compatible with a strict adherence to SMART criteria. In 2010, Dr Penny Lacey, of Birmingham University's School of Education, produced SCRUFFY (student-led, creative, unspecified, fun for youngsters) targets to highlight how people at early levels of development learn, focusing on the difference between skill- or task-based activities (where progress is supposedly linear) and the complex learning which underpins social communication and interaction (this is discussed further in Chapters 3 and 7 and in Hewett, 2012).

Indeed, anyone who enters an Intensive Interaction session with a SMART target in mind, such as 'Andrew will respond eight times during an Intensive Interaction session lasting ten minutes by giving the adult eye contact and smiling', is doomed to failure. What if the child only responds seven times and it is coming up to the ninth minute – will the practitioner push for that last response and the session no longer be child-led? What about if the response is not by eye contact or smiles but by stilling, vocalising, or moving a finger or foot? This is why the phrase 'outcome led, not target driven' is the guiding mantra of Intensive Interaction, mirroring its principles.

We can adapt the notion of SMART-ness when considering Intensive Interaction outcomes. 'Specific' will relate to learning the FoCs, although we will not predict the exact way this learning will be evidenced by the learner; 'measurable' will relate to how we can tell that the child has met, or is progressing towards, the outcome rather than setting any pre-determined numerically based targets; 'achievable' and 'realistic' will relate to the outcome being 'within their reach', remembering that it takes numerous repetitions to consolidate, and even then the outcome will not necessarily remain static due to the process of spiralling (Hewett et al., 2012, p. 79); 'time-bound' relates to the outcomes generally being set by Key Stage and broken down into smaller steps that are reviewed annually. The complex learning involved in the gradual development of the FoCs means that we cannot predict a specific time-scale, and it may well be a life-long development. This should be taken into account during the Annual Review Process.

## Intensive Interaction outcomes should

- Focus on the development of the FoCs as a priority area of learning.
- Describe the anticipated learning outcomes based on the FoCs.
- Describe the impact of the FoCs on underpinning communication skills, supporting social interaction, building relationships, etc.
- Allow the individual to express development of the FoCs in their own way.
- Be 'within the individual's reach' by building on their current repertoire.

Above all, avoid reducing these complex learning processes to numerical statements or 'tick boxes'.

### Note about using the attainment framework statements for EHC Plan outcomes

The Attainment Framework (Firth, 2004) is often referenced as a useful tool for demonstrating progress relating to social engagement, so the question arises, are they a suitable fit for EHC Plans? Where I found examples of these being used, the EHC Plan used one of the Attainment Framework levels as a step (or short-term aim) towards an outcome in Section E.

For example:

*Nicole will consistently demonstrate the Attention and Response level during Intensive Interaction sessions (The student or client begins to respond (although not consistently) to what is happening in an interactive episode e.g. by showing signs of surprise, enjoyment, frustration or dissatisfaction).*

There are various risks with using the Attainment Framework in this way. The Attainment Framework 'identifies the level of involvement demonstrated by the person rather than the actual skill set used' (Barber and Firth, 2011, pp. 102–103). Using a level of the framework to set a 'target/outcome' may fail to take account of the breadth of the development associated with the FoCs and how they occur.

Additionally, this runs the risk of becoming a 'tick-box' exercise, where a pupil who is seen to have 'achieved' the attainment level a predetermined number of times is then moved up to the next level. This then also raises the question of linearity – by using the Attainment Framework in this way, are we suggesting that we expect a linear model of progression, which is in opposition to what we know about how learning happens in early development? It would be relatively natural to assume a pupil would move between several stages of the Attainment Framework, perhaps even within a single session, depending on their emotional state and environment, and possibly many other factors. This is clearly acknowledged in the latest statutory assessment document, 'The Standards and Testing Agency's Engagement Model', which states: 'Often these pupils do not make progress in a linear way. . . . Progress for these pupils can also be variable. They may . . . plateau or lose some of the gains they have made, before progress starts again' (Standards and Testing Agency, 2020, p. 23).

This also relates directly to the spiral model (see visual representation of the spiral model in Chapter 4) taken from the work of Dr Dave Hewett and offers a good visual representation of what progress might look like with the FoCs, highlighting the importance of repetition and progressing 'onwards and upwards . . . staying in one place, . . . perhaps spiralling down a few loops . . . during times of stress or adverse circumstances for the person" (Hewett, 2012, p. 151). (Further discussion of ways in which children learn at this early developmental stage can be found in Chapter 4.)

# Writing Intensive Interaction outcomes for the EHC Plan – Section F

This should be detailed, specific, and quantified, for example, the type, hours, frequency of support, and level of expertise (including where this support is secured through a personal budget), and should clearly support achievement of the identified outcomes (DfE, 2015, pp. 164, 166). Intensive Interaction should be included as the provision for all special educational needs (Section B) relating to the development of the FoCs 1 and 2.

While the learning involved in communicating and interacting socially is complex, the provision needed to support this development is relatively simple: regular, frequent, and high-quality Intensive Interaction activities with members of staff trained in the approach.

Education, Health and Care Plans

> Information to include:
>
> - Techniques staff need to adopt (tuning-in, following their lead, pausing, responsive style, sense of minimalism, being available, mutual enjoyment).
> - Frequency of Intensive Interaction opportunities combining spontaneous and regular timetabled sessions.
> - The need for ongoing staff training, mentoring, and continuing professional development by suitably experienced and qualified trainers.
> - How Intensive Interaction supports development of the identified need and outcome.
> - Intensive Interaction must be referenced by name.

Example from EHC Plan, including Sections A, B, E, and F.

In practical terms this might look like this:

Table 13.1 Examples of wordings for EHC Plan, Sections A, B, E, and F.

| Section A | Section B | Section E | Section F |
|---|---|---|---|
| One Page Profile.<br><br>'I am beginning to enjoy Intensive Interaction with familiar members of staff'.<br><br>'If I am feeling distressed, Intensive Interaction can help me connect with those around me: help me by stepping back, getting lower down (if safe), staying tuned-in, and remember pauses may be longer than usual as I process everything going on around me'. | **Communication and Interaction:** strengths and achievements.<br><br>Andrew's use of appropriate eye contact is developing. Particularly when engaged in Intensive Interaction, Andrew can give eye contact happily and comfortably for short periods. He is starting to use facial expressions to show his different emotions including happiness, sadness, excitement, and frustration. | For Andrew to develop FOCs to underpin his communication skills.<br><br>For Andrew to develop his joint attention skills so that he can access basic social and learning opportunities.<br><br>For Andrew to develop his language and communication skills so that he can:<br>- Make his needs and ideas known.<br>- Respond to the interactions of others.<br>- Initiate interactions with peers. | Andrew will be supported by staff who understand Andrew's communication difficulties and are skilled in Intensive Interaction strategies to develop Andrew's grasp of the FoCs. (SENCo to identify staff training needs and liaise with relevant professionals.) Andrew will have access to Intensive Interaction through incidental opportunities throughout the day and specific identified sessions during the week. |

(Continued)

Table 13.1 Continued

| Section A | Section B | Section E | Section F |
|---|---|---|---|
| | **Special educational needs:** Andrew shows little awareness of those around him and moves around in what staff describe as his own 'bubble'. | | |
| | ***Social, emotional, and mental health:*** strengths and achievements. Andrew is starting to develop early signs of self-moderation of his behaviour during Intensive Interaction sessions. When the adult withdraws attention for brief periods if he is becoming very excited, he is able to regulate his arousal levels effectively. **Special educational needs:** Andrew generally plays alone. He is starting to show a fleeting interest in other children and familiar adults but does not yet tolerate them sharing his personal space. | For Andrew to begin to respond to others so that he can ultimately develop his ability to play with peers. For Andrew to develop an understanding of different emotions, including happy, sad, cross, excited, surprised, and worried. | Andrew will begin to learn the Fundamentals of Communication through Intensive Interaction, including enjoyment of being with and sharing space with others and starting to build positive relationships with familiar adults. Andrew will be supported by his staff team to start 'in the moment' learning about his feelings while experiencing a range of emotions during Intensive Interaction sessions. |

# Supporting Intensive Interaction documentation across a school setting

Once I had established the guidelines for documenting Intensive Interaction within EHC Plans, the challenge was to explore how to maximise my reach across my school setting and to support my colleagues to document progress where possible.

If we only consider that which we can physically do ourselves, (e.g. the EHC Plans where we can directly contribute or the children with whom we work directly), then we will always be limited to those pupils we know on an individual basis.

In my role as Coordinator, it is important to consider how to support and mentor others to document Intensive Interaction to ensure it is available to all those who need it.

# Supporting and enabling other professionals to include Intensive Interaction within Education, Health and Care Plans

I see my role as supporting my colleagues in the following three ways:

### Education: ensure staff are aware of the need to reference Intensive Interaction in EHC Plans

It is essential to ensure that other professionals, including all teachers within the setting, are aware of the importance of Intensive Interaction (and the FoCs), and therefore the need to reference it within EHC Plans. We must ensure that the development of the FoCs is considered as a priority for our pupils.

My goals around this are to:

- Reference EHC Plans within induction sessions (for teachers, outreach staff, teaching assistants).
- Reiterate during 'Annual Intensive Interaction Refresher' sessions the foundational nature of the FoCs and their impact on other areas of learning and development.
- Deliver Intensive Interaction 'refresher' training sessions for all classes including those with high numbers of verbal pupils.
- Liaise with other professionals contributing to EHC Plans (for example, speech and language therapy team).

**Table 13.2** Detail of a structure to support professionals to include Intensive Interaction in EHC Plans.

| When | Topic | Who |
|---|---|---|
| Staff meeting time allocated for Intensive Interaction | Examples and guidelines on referencing Intensive Interaction within One Page Profiles included within EHC Plan Section A<br><br>Action: amend and update One Page Profiles as necessary | Whole class team familiar with pupils to contribute |
| Teacher's meeting | Training session to be delivered to cover:<br><br>- identification of pupils who need Intensive Interaction on EHC Plan (to include pupils with speech).<br>- outline guiding principles for EHC Plans and Intensive Interaction.<br>- examples of writing needs, outcomes, and provision to reflect Intensive Interaction.<br><br>Action: identify a pupil with upcoming Annual Review who has a need for Intensive Interaction. Review and amend EHC Plan as needed to reflect this need considering guidance. | Teachers |

### Support and guidance: offer staff teams ongoing support and guidance with updating their EHC Plans to include Intensive Interaction

I set up a system to structure this process, identifying the level of involvement of different groups of staff and how, and when, I would deliver this support.

### Influencing a whole-school policy and approach to Intensive Interaction

It is important to ensure the Coordinator's role and expectation for including Intensive Interaction within EHC Plans is embedded within school documentation.

One of the ways to support writing Intensive Interaction into EHC Plans is to set out the expectations within school documents, including my role in supporting this. This can be in policies, rationales, and all other relevant documentation. As with any plans for change, it is a good idea to share this information with the senior leadership team and get them on board!

> Here is an example of my expectations around EHC Plans within our school Intensive Interaction rationale:
>
> *'Developing the ability to engage in social interaction is a priority area of learning for all our pupils. To be able to engage in social interaction means developing a set of skills referred to as the Fundamentals of Communication (see Chapter 3).*
>
> *All pupils who have not yet developed the Fundamentals of Communication (FoCs) should have this reflected in their EHC Plan. As the FoCs relate to social interaction, rather than functional speech, this includes those pupils who have established speech, but who still struggle with being able to use the FoCs to interact on a social level. Intensive Interaction Coordinator, Lucy Hankin, will give further support and advice for EHC Plans referencing Intensive Interaction'.*

## Supporting the Annual Review process – discussion of progress towards outcomes

There is a need to educate the way in which progress occurs in Intensive Interaction; it is an important aspect of supporting colleagues. It is crucial for practitioners to avoid any attempt to conform to a tick-box culture or methods that promote linear or simplistic notions of assessing progress towards outcomes. It is also essential for teachers to be supported to 'talk the talk' around Intensive Interaction (e.g. regarding spiralling progress) when describing progress to parents at Annual Reviews and to use the correct terminology to describe the very real progress that students are making. It is well established that progress occurs gradually as a result of many repetitions (Hewett et al., 2012, p. 81) and that it may take days, weeks, months, or even a lifetime for FoCs to become truly embedded.

## Concluding remarks

As Intensive Interaction practitioners, we all share a common aim: to get Intensive Interaction out there to as many individuals as we can, enabling greater numbers to benefit from this approach. EHC Plans, as legal documents, are proving themselves as essential in this process, with well-written plans ensuring individuals have access to good quality Intensive Interaction provision every day, embedded throughout their curriculum. A key aspect of the EHC Plan is to prepare a young person for adulthood, and as such it is essential to include Intensive Interaction from the beginning and for this to remain part of the EHC Plan throughout their education and beyond. We know an individual's need for Intensive Interaction is not limited to their years within the education system but reaches far beyond that time. EHC Plans that document the critical nature of Intensive Interaction for an individual, particularly in preparing for adulthood, should help to secure this provision across future transitions and placements.

## References

Barber, M. and Firth, G. (2011). *Using Intensive Interaction with a Person with a Social or Communicative Impairment*. London: Jessica Kingsley Publishers.

Delivering Better Outcomes Together Consortium, (n.d.). *Developing Outcomes in EHC Plans*. Available at: www.sendpathfinder.co.uk/delivering-better-outcomes-together [Accessed 10 February 2021].

Department for Education (DfE) and Department for Health (DoH), (2015). *Special Educational Needs and Disabilities Code of Practice: 0–25 Years*. Available at: www.gov.uk/government/publications/send-code-of-practice-0-to-25 [Accessed 9 February 2021].

Firth, G. (2004). *A Framework for Recognising Attainment in Intensive Interaction*. Leeds: Mental Health NHS Trust.

Hewett, D. (2012). 'What is Intensive Interaction? Curriculum, process and approach'. In: D. Hewett, ed., *Intensive Interaction: Theoretical Perspectives*. London: Sage Publications, pp. 137–154.

Hewett, D., Firth, G., Barber, M. and Harrison, T. (2012). *The Intensive Interaction Handbook*. London: Sage Publications.

Lacey, P. (2010). Smart and scruffy targets. *SLD Experience*, 57, pp. 16–21.

Nind, M. and Hewett, D. (2001). *A Practical Guide to Intensive Interaction*. Kidderminster: British Institute of Learning Disabilities.

Standards and Testing Agency (STA), (2016). *The Rochford Review: Final Report Review of Assessment for Pupils Working Below the Standard of National Curriculum Tests*. Available at: https://assets.publishing.service.gov.uk/government/uploads/system/uploads/attachment_data/file/561411/Rochford_Review_Report_v5_PFDA.pdf [Accessed 10 February 2021].

Standards and Testing Agency (STA), (2020). *The Engagement Model: Guidance for Maintained Schools, Academies (Including Free Schools) and Local Authorities*. Available at: www.government/publications/the-engagement-model [Accessed 9 February 2021].

# 14. Getting it right with recording Intensive Interaction

*Ian Harris and Pam Smith*

## Introduction

After all the chapters describing Intensive Interaction in so many different contexts, it seems right to end the book with how we capture all the wonderful progress that has been discussed. There is a familiar adage which says, 'If it isn't written down it didn't happen'. This chapter therefore discusses ways of observing, defining, capturing, and recording Intensive Interaction progress, including information about a bespoke online tool for Recording Intensive Interaction Outcomes (RIIO). The discussion encompasses good practice and considerations around recording Intensive Interaction and explores ways of ensuring that the intangible, qualitative nature of Intensive Interaction is not lost.

## How the development of the Fundamentals of Communication calls for re-thinking traditional ways of recording outcomes

As a process-central approach (see Chapter 4 and Chapter 10) we must always be mindful of the mantra that Intensive Interaction is 'outcome led, not target driven'. Being process-central, the outcomes emerge over time, and whilst we can have some broad ideas about what the learning outcomes might be – for example, we will know when a child is just beginning to recognise and tolerate a person in their space as opposed to starting to initiate interactions – with Intensive Interaction we do not set targets because it does not reflect the reality of the learning taking place.

> When attempting to capture and record the outcomes in the Fundamentals of Communication (FoCs – Nind and Hewett, 1994) with our students, it quickly becomes apparent that their complexity does not fit into a convenient tick box–style, mechanical process. Neither can it always be expressed adequately in writing – emotions are hard to describe using language and become diminished in the attempt. 'Harry smiled at me' does not capture the joy of that interaction and the

DOI: 10.4324/9781003170839-14

> unique moment of deep connectivity that occurred between you. 'Lawrence allowed me to take turns singing words in his favourite song' does not capture how he gave permission, what a huge step forward this was for him, and the complex adjustments of position and proximity that conveyed his acceptance of you in his space.

Recording progress with the FoCs can be a minefield. An inexperienced practitioner may miss subtle changes in expressivity, be unaware of the significance of an event, or forget to note something because they are called away urgently to attend to another child and the 'busyness' of the day takes over. There may be inconsistency in recording purely through individual subjectivity. In Chapter 6, the author describes the Intensive Interaction Coordinator's essential role in training teams to work together to develop an informed eye and common parlance when describing what they see; and the importance of practice, consistency, and insight into the development of the FoCs. People may need a 'buddy' to help them develop confidence in their recording skills. Although this buddy system may initially be time consuming and appear costly, in the long run this investment pays dividends.

Schools are driven by the need for assessment. Data plays a major role in Ofsted inspections, and teachers are rightly accountable for their students' progress for reporting to local authorities, parents, governing bodies, and as part of their appraisals. Assessment and recording progress are seen as essential for setting appropriate targets to meet children's needs and satisfy legal requirements of their Education, Health and Care (EHC) Plans (see Chapter 13). Leadership teams may hold meetings to discuss half-yearly and end-of-year assessments with teachers; and if a child has made less than the predicted progress, they are required to justify why that has not occurred. In this culture it is no wonder that people prefer quantitative data that can show a nice straight line of someone who could previously count to five now being able to count to ten or matching six pictures instead of three.

> But communication and social-communication development is a messy business and far from linear (Hewett, 2012). The process of spiralling has been mentioned frequently throughout this book, and uneven progress or even deterioration in skills is fully recognised within the Engagement Model (Standards and Testing Agency – STA, 2020), so we need to consider the purpose of recording and who it is for, namely to ensure that we are meeting the needs of the individual student.

Intensive Interaction is built around the person and depends upon the practitioner having a full, deep, and holistic knowledge of them as an individual. This is a valid reason for gathering as much information as we can about them to build up a picture of who they are, what they can do, and how we can support them through using the wonderful processes discussed in this book, to learn and keep developing the FoCs. The individual is at the centre of the process, supporting the principle of the Rochford Review (Rochford, 2016) that 'Every pupil should be able to demonstrate his or her attainment'. Therefore, if we read their paperwork, it should reflect where they are as an individual within their learning, not simply a tick list – they are far more than this, as we all know!

Before considering the practicalities of recording progress it might be useful to consider more about relationships and their incongruity with target setting. This beautiful testimony to Intensive Interaction was written by a parent about his experience with his son.

> George's dad writes:
>
> *'I wanted to share something with you.*
>
> *I just had the most incredible hour with George, my six-year-old son who has severe autism. He hasn't been sleeping well for months. The last few weeks have been very bad with very little sleep and him really battling at school. Today things peaked with him really scratching the teachers and other pupils in his class because he was so over aroused (one of the teachers had a big plaster on their face) and he was completely hyper in his swimming lesson after school when the water usually calms him.*
>
> *At 18.45 he was still very hyper, jumping up and down on his mini trampoline and vocalising loudly. I was braced for yet another very late night. By 20.00 he was peacefully asleep in bed.*
>
> *So, what happened in that hour. We sat in the bath, with our faces about 10cm away from each other for forty minutes and vocalised to each other (I mimicked him and replied to him), shared hand gestures and just looked at each other. I felt like I was connecting with him in a way that I have never done and was looking deep into his soul. Now I get Intensive Interaction! These little children want what we all want – deep connection, to be understood, to be heard, and to form deep bonds with those closest to us. One thing I realised today is that I need to be in a calm and sorted emotional space myself so that when I connect with him, he is able to sense that calmness and really connect with it and feel that the world is safe and ok even if he doesn't feel like that in himself in the beginning.'*

The only measurables mentioned in this beautiful and incredibly moving piece are 10 cm face distance and 40-minute duration. If we wrote a target specifying 'George will sit in a bath with his Dad with their faces at a distance of 10 cms for 40 minutes', we could give it a great big tick! However, in no way would that sum up even a tiny fragment of all the wonderful emotional and social learning that was going on in that interaction. George's dad speaks about looking deep into his soul. We all know what that feels like with our special children. But try putting that into a target!

# Recording Intensive Interaction outcomes

## Video recording

The starting point for Intensive Interaction is always observation – using notes and video (see Chapter 6). Video recordings are an essential tool, allowing us to see things that we may miss in the moment and to improve and reflect upon our own practice. They are also the most powerful evidence of progress that you will keep on each individual. Barber (2018) describes in detail best practice in setting up video shots (especially when filming both the practitioner and the individual), and it is worth trying these out in advance by filming your colleagues to get this right.

There are several additional challenges around videoing besides getting the right shot. Staff may be embarrassed and self-conscious about being videoed – focusing on the student and lots of practice helps to reduce this. There are also practical problems, such as finding a member of staff free to video; having the video equipment to hand (that will not be a magnet for the other students!); finding time to download and analyse clips both individually and as a team; and finding ways of editing, storing, and labelling videos (to avoid a drive full of random unedited films). Above all, finding ways of incorporating Intensive Interaction progress into standardised assessment tools and sharing videos at parent meetings and reviews. These will all need to be considered and brainstormed within your teams and with your management team. For this to work and be sustainable, many schools who have successfully embedded Intensive Interaction have a full-time Intensive Interaction Coordinator who trains and supports colleagues and liaises with management to fulfill requirements at all levels (see the Intensive Interaction Institute website and Chapter 6).

## Using videos alongside written records

When Intensive Interaction sessions begin to get established, best practice around recording sessions should always combine written and video recording. Best practice suggests that half termly videos are a good way to track progress. But also be prepared for ad hoc moments that need to be recorded and have the video camera (or whatever device you choose to use) close to hand and in 'grabbable' distance!

> Written recording will also aim to capture significant planned (i.e. timetabled) and unplanned (i.e. spontaneous) Intensive Interaction moments. They may be:
>
> - In the moment: scribbling a hasty Post-it note recognising something new and amazing – 'Aisha came and took my hand to initiate a game' – and putting it on the child's Wow board.

- Session notes: there are a range of options for these, and it is worth exploring which work best for your team. For example, significant Intensive Interaction events for individuals can be recorded using session recording sheets (see Chapter 5), New Developments sheets (see Appendix 4) into which you can write or type, or Monthly Progress Trackers (see example in Chapter 5).

Challenges around written recording include ensuring the sheets are readily available for individual staff and clearly labelled with the individual's name; giving time for staff to fill these in after sessions and supporting staff who find it difficult or forget to record sessions due to lack of confidence. Simple suggestions such as having individual clipboards with pens attached; not expecting staff to fill in recording sheets during breaks or after school; and offering regular support – some form of ongoing/ mentorship can make a big difference. Team meetings should be set aside to discuss any issues with filling in forms or celebrate achievements so that staff feel they are making a difference in their students' social communication, which will in turn reinforce their Intensive Interaction practice. Use these times to pick up on what individual staff members are doing well and comment on their style: 'I really liked the way you waited for Jack to respond during that session and gave him time to process'. Using a 'Style Sheet' (see Appendix 5) can be a great way of evaluating videos (see Chapter 6) but also, please mention it if you just see someone with great practice in the corner of the classroom or in the playground. It can make all the difference to their confidence and self-development as an Intensive Interaction practitioner.

At some point, all the information from Post-it notes and recording sheets will have to be gathered and reported on, at termly or half-yearly Parents Evenings and Annual Reviews of students' EHC Plans. At this point it is essential to link the child's learning to the FoCs and areas of learning outlined by the EHC Plan. Teachers will inevitably wish they had a simpler way of doing this, and there may be some light at the end of the tunnel!

## Online recording – RIIO

In 2018 research carried out by Hewett and Calveley substantiated the need for a reporting tool, the results of which are documented in 'The Intensive Interaction Outcomes Reporter' (Calveley, 2018). RIIO (Recording Intensive Interaction Outcomes) builds on this by developing the original tool's structure and content and making it into an online relational database. While the term 'relational database' may appear daunting, the important thing to know about RIIO is that it is easy to use and yet powerful in what it can produce. Although it is being considered here in the context of classroom educational settings, RIIO can follow the individual and can be transported beyond childhood and into adult settings. This makes it an invaluable tool in enabling continuity for the benefit of the learner.

# RIIO, the Rochford Review and the Engagement Model

Over the past few years the government has been reviewing education and what it means for students working below the Key Stages of the National Curriculum (Department for Education, DfE, 2014). This in turn has put into context how RIIO fits in with those trends in a way that recognises Intensive Interaction as an appropriate approach to learning.

The Rochford Review (2016) made a number of recommendations about the assessment of learners working below the Key Stages of the National Curriculum in non-subject-specific areas. These included planned implementations as a result of the government's response (DfE, 2017):

- Replacement of P scales by assessment of the four areas of need defined by the SEND Code of Practice (cognition and learning, communication and interaction, social, emotional and mental health, sensory and/or physical) using the seven aspects of engagement defined by the Complex Learning Difficulties and Disabilities (CLDD) research group (Specialist Schools and Academies Trust, 2011).
- Individual schools to devise appropriate, flexible methods of assessment which will show the unique, uneven profiles of learners, their different learning pathways, and lateral, non-linear learning as well as linear progress.
- Sharing such assessments with staff, parents, carers and between organisations, providing evidence of accountability as well as meeting statutory requirements.
- Collaboration between schools, pro-active sharing of good practice, engaging in innovative research, and including training in this kind of assessment in initial teacher training and CPD to improve teachers' confidence in these areas.

The Engagement Model arose from recommendations made by the Rochford Review (2016) and the Standards and Testing Agency Pilot (STA, 2018). It is a multi-dimensional, child-centred approach focusing on students' abilities, recognising complexity, and encouraging the sharing of information. The Engagement Model is based on regular observational assessment and reflective pedagogy. It encourages a continuous cycle of assessment, planning, action, and evaluation, identifying a student's progress against each area of engagement in conjunction with their EHC Plan. It is flexible and holistic and can be used as part of the school's existing frameworks. Schools do not have to submit data to the DfE about progress, only identify which pupils are being assessed by this method.

> The Engagement Model (STA, 2020) includes five non-hierarchical areas of engagement:
>
> - Exploration – identifying stimuli and objects of interest, showing curiosity, using these in different contexts.

> - Realisation – interaction with new stimuli or activities or new aspects of familiar stimuli or objects, attempts at control, using new skills, or knowledge in different contexts.
> - Anticipation – making predictions or associations, interpreting cues or prompts, understanding cause and effect.
> - Persistence – sustaining attention, attempts to interact, intentional changes applying skills and knowledge.
> - Initiation – spontaneity, independent action without direction, different ways to investigate, understanding how to create an impact.

The Engagement Model includes detailed guidelines on observation which have much in common with Intensive Interaction principles of tuning in and being fully focused on the individual. The draft guidance explains (p. 13):

*When observing a pupil, teachers may look for subtle nuances of response and behaviour.*

**These might include:**

- *fleeting eye movements or pupil dilation*
- *'stilling' (a momentary freeze)*
- *a small change in breathing pattern*
- *tensing or relaxing*
- *a small change in posture*
- *a change in facial expression*
- *vocalisation*
- *a movement of the mouth, hands or feet*

The guidance recommends using photographs, video, and IT-based solutions to record evidence, assisting with time management and the effectiveness of assessments, and ensuring evidence is easily and securely stored, retrieved, and shared, as collaboration is in the interests of the student. This is the primary purpose of RIIO, and although RIIO has been developed for the benefit of Intensive Interaction practitioners it is designed to mesh with the requirements of the Engagement Model.

These categories may look strange to classroom practitioners, as they do not map directly onto the four SEND areas of an individual's EHC Plan and therefore their Individual Learning Plans/Individual Education Plans (ILP/IEP) – which may form the centre of their curriculum. However, students who are at the earliest stages of learning are likely to be focusing principally upon developing the FoCs at the centre of their curriculum, as these are the essential precursors to learning. Therefore, their main learning will be in the

> RIIO allows the recording of dated individual observations of Intensive Interaction sessions with links to video and other documentary evidence. In RIIO, the FoCs have been divided into four categories encompassing social, cognitive, emotional, and physical learning. These categories are deeply interconnected and not mutually exclusive. Broadly speaking, the FoCs 1 map onto social and cognitive aspects; and FoCs 2 map onto emotional learning. Physical responses were added as part of the Outcomes Reporter, and these have been retained in RIIO because they highlight the importance of self-awareness only touched upon elsewhere in the FoCs. The overall record is holistic, but individual observations can record variable and non-linear progress.

area of communication and interaction. As explained in Chapter 13, as an individual's learning begins to expand, the FoCs can be extended to be included in each of these four areas of SEND. For some students with social-communication difficulties, the learning of the FoCs will continue to run alongside their learning, even if they reach National Curriculum levels in their subject learning. The statements included in RIIO cannot and should not be used to set targets for a child's EHC Plan or ILP/IEP or as a rigid assessment framework but, rather, to record emergent outcomes.

While these four areas do not map onto the areas of learning from the EHC Plan that need to be identified, recorded, and reported upon as part of Annual Reviews, RIIO offers opportunities to record detailed progress in the FoCs that may not be recorded elsewhere but may be essential learning for the individual. For example, recording observations of eye movements and changes in facial expression to show increased social awareness and responsiveness and the ability to sustain shared attention, which is needed for all learning.

The actual location of recorded observations within RIIO is decided by the practitioner's professional judgement as to which area of development it represents. Similarly, the practitioner would use their professional judgement to decide to what extent the observation is evidence of one or more of the five engagement areas in the Engagement Model of assessment.

RIIO is still under development for education establishments. Schools are currently contributing to see if ways can be developed to combine the observations and evidence collected in RIIO with their current assessment systems. This would support the aim of the Engagement Model guidance around time management, effective assessment, access, storage, and retrieval. As stated, the Rochford Review 'recognises the importance of schools engaging in research to support good practice'. Being involved in further research and development into the efficacy of RIIO would meet these criteria (see the Recording Intensive Interaction Outcomes website www.riio.uk/ for further details).

## Concluding remarks

Recording progress in Intensive Interaction is essential to capture tiny steps of learning as they happen within sessions. As a process-central approach based upon emergent outcomes rather than target setting, it is essential to gather evidence that progress occurs in line with access to practising the FoCs multiple times with skilled, responsive communicative partners. Current good practice advocates for use of video evidence, recording sheets and is moving towards the inclusion of evidence on the RIIO online platform. Work is ongoing to find ways to mesh these with schools' own assessment procedures and online platforms.

RIIO is designed as an aid to Intensive Interaction practitioners, enabling them to record and share their observations of progress and development within Intensive Interaction sessions. The precise observations are backed up by video evidence, which record the unique pathways of individual progress in a way that could usefully contribute to the new type of flexible assessment that the Rochford Review and the Engagement Model recommends.

RIIO contributes significantly to the adoption of the Engagement Model of assessment to be used in primary and secondary education. The evidence gathered for Intensive Interaction purposes, if computerised to be readily available and accessible for sharing, can also provide evidence for accountability to parents, carers, and Ofsted (i.e. proof that areas beyond cognitive learning are being addressed by teachers). This evidence can also be shared with new organisations if the individual moves schools or can follow them beyond education into adult services.

## References

Barber, M. (2018). 'Recording the activities and maintaining the processes'. In: D. Hewett, ed., *The Intensive Interaction Handbook*, 2nd ed. London: Sage Publications, pp. 85–105.

Calveley, J. (2018). 'The Intensive Interaction outcomes reporter'. In: D. Hewett, ed., *The Intensive Interaction Handbook*, 2nd ed. London: Sage Publications, pp. 107–111.

Department for Education (DfE), (2014). *The National Curriculum in England Framework Document*. Available at: https://assets.publishing.service.gov.uk/government/uploads/system/uploads/attachment_data/file/381344/Master_final_national_curriculum_28_Nov.pdf [Accessed 17 February 2021].

Department for Education (DfE), (2017). *Primary School Pupil Assessment: Rochford Review Recommendations Government Consultation Response*. Available at: https://assets.publishing.service.gov.uk/government/uploads/system/uploads/attachment_data/file/644729/Rochford_consultation_response.pdf [Accessed 16 May 2021].

Hewett, D. (2012). 'What is Intensive Interaction? Curriculum, process and approach'. In: D. Hewett, ed., *Intensive Interaction: Theoretical Perspectives*. London: Sage Publications, pp. 137–154.

Nind, M. and Hewett, D. (1994). *Access to Communication: Developing the Basics of Communication with People with Severe Learning Difficulties Through Intensive Interaction*. London: David Fulton.

Rochford, D. (2016). *The Rochford Review: Final Report Review of Assessment for Pupils Working Below the Standard of National Curriculum Tests*. London: The Stationery Office.

Specialist Schools and Academies Trust, (2011). *The Complex Learning Difficulties and Disabilities Research Project, Developing Pathways to Personalised Learning: Final Report*. Available at: http://complexneeds.org.uk/modules/Module-3.2-Engaging-in-learning–key-approaches/All/downloads/m10p010d/the_complex_learning_difficulties.pdf [Accessed 17 February 2021].

Standards and Testing Agency (STA), (2018). *Piloting the 7 Aspects of Engagement for Summative Assessment: Qualitative Evaluation*. Available at: www.gov.uk/government/publications/7-aspects-of-engagement-pilot-qualitative-evaluation [Accessed 17 February 2021].

Standards and Testing Agency, (2020). *The Engagement Model: Guidance for Maintained Schools, Academies (Including Free Schools) and Local Authorities*. Available at: www.government/publications/the-engagement-model [Accessed 17 February 2021].

# Appendix 1
## Video observation sheet

Name:		Date:		Time:		Venue:

| | |
|---|---|
| Do you start to see things about the person in the videos that you did not notice with real-life observations? What are they? | |
| In particular, what do you notice about what she/he does with her/his eyes – where she/he looks? How frequently? | |
| Do you notice anything more about the person's face? The range of facial expressions the person has? | |
| How about the person's body language and posture? Do you notice anything more about how she/he moves? | |
| Do you think you can see the person's contentment or anxiety more clearly on video? | |
| Does the video more clearly display things about staff movements or interactions? | |
| Other thoughts? | |

# Appendix 2
## Summary of observations

### Having completed your observations, use this sheet to summarise what you have learnt

What have you learnt about things the person likes?

What have you learnt about things the person does not like?

What have you learnt about how the person spends most of her/his time?

What have you learnt about the person's reaction to other people?

What have you learnt about the person's communication abilities?

What have you learnt about things you could respond to or join in with when interacting?

Anything else?

# Appendix 3
# A value charter for schools

Clearly setting out a school's ethos is essential in guaranteeing that a social model is being implemented and that an aspiration to maximise the children's quality of life and well-being is at the core of shared organisational values. In education, this means that not only buildings but the curriculum and whole school environment should be accessible to learners' individual and diverse profiles. Adopting a document that conveys a school's philosophy and belief system will support the implementation of Intensive Interaction, stating some general educational standards and principles that members of staff subscribe to, which define the school's collective culture and community mindset.

Any such document must be a concise reminder of the school's ethos. It can also potentially provide a basis for induction training, thereby ensuring everyone shares the same understanding and philosophy as well as protecting the integrity of Intensive Interaction.

## Core and intrinsic values – specimen document

We aim to support each student to reach their full potential as a person. By this, we mean encouraging their:

- Uniqueness
- Individuality
- Expression
- Sense of agency
- Thought
- Creativity
- Curiosity
- Passions
- Emotional experience
- Cognition
- Physicality
- Relationship

Humans are social beings, and human contact is essential for well-being.

*Our values determine our 'Code of Conduct'*

### Expectations around our students:
- Each student is a valued individual.
- We accept every student as they are whilst desiring for them to be the best version of themselves that they can be.
- Each student is much more than their behaviour and external presentation.
- Each student has a state of inner being which is also the concern of the practitioner.

- Each student's state of security (inner peace) and well-being will be enhanced by proper access to meaningful, understandable communication and relationship.
- We do not understand everything about why a student presents or behaves as they do, and we do not know what it is like to be another person. Therefore, we will not constrain them from being as they are.
- We accord students the dignity of not placing unrealistic expectations on them.
- We respect every student as a whole person who experiences the full range of human feelings and emotions.

## Inclusion in social activity

- A priority for human everyday life is communication and the access this gives to connecting with others and having positive relationships.
- Social communication is essential for well-being: sense of self, good self-esteem, psychological health, and general well-being are largely dependent on having secure and responsive relationships and extensive opportunities for social communication. Therefore, each student should get access to sufficient supply of purely social 'chit-chat' throughout the day, every day.
- The first outcome of an Intensive Interaction activity is the interaction – that is, that the practitioner connects with the learner and that verbal or non-verbal communication occurs conveying mutual enjoyment.

## Embracing the Intensive Interaction philosophy

- Intensive Interaction adopts an attitude of expectancy but not expectation. This means it is assumed that the person may have more ability to communicate than is immediately apparent but that there is no pressure or expectation for performance of any particular skill.
- Intensive Interaction can bring about beneficial effects for staff and the team, particularly regarding morale, work satisfaction, sense of achievement, motivation and experiencing better relationships.
- The best progress occurs when there are frequent opportunities for Intensive Interaction activities to take place and that any and all outcomes are allowed to gradually emerge.

## Expectations for staff, students, and parents

We start from the premise that:

- Everyone (by 'everyone' we mean students, staff, and parents) is doing the best that they can.
- We will not make anyone's life more difficult or more painful.
- We will do all we can to help everyone to develop within their personal potential.
- We will not subject anyone to things that we cannot explain/defend/back up.
- We will not make anyone do things that they do not want to do without respecting their freedom of expression and free will.

# Appendix 4
## Intensive Interaction: new development form

*Please fill in if you see the student do something you have never seen them do before.*

**Name**: Banu Gulek         **Class:** Purple Class

**Communication Outcome from ILP**: Banu will begin to initiate interactions with a familiar adult.

| Date/ where | What happened | Staff |
|---|---|---|
| 14/9/20 Purple Class | Held up foot so that I could give it a squeeze. Looked fleetingly towards me and smiled. | Pam |
| 17/9/20 Soft Play | Giggled when I blew a raspberry on her foot! | Pam |
| 22/9/20 Purple Class Garden Area | Came to join me on trampette and initiated game of scratching the canvas. Looked towards me when I joined in. Lots of nice pauses and re-initiation. | Heather |
| | | |
| | | |
| | | |
| | | |
| | | |
| | | |

# Appendix 5
# Style/technique list

| Video of: | Date: |
|---|---|
| Available look | |
| Available self/body | |
| Positioning | |
| Observes | |
| Tunes in | |
| Relaxed | |
| Enjoyment | |
| Unhurried | |
| Does not drive on | |
| Pauses | |
| Waits | |
| Doesn't do too much | |
| Responsive | |
| Timing/tempo/pace/flow | |
| Ways of responding | |
| Responds to vocalisations | |

## Style/technique list

| Video of: | Date: |
|---|---|
| Responds with running commentary | |
| Joins in | |
| Imitates | |
| Use of touch | |
| Finds the right moment to develop, build, extend | |
| Uses Scenario 2 when right | |
| Anything else? Comments | |

# Glossary

**Affordance/Novel affordance:** the quality or property of an object that defines its possible uses. The term was originally coined by the American psychologist James Gibson.

**Agency:** the idea that people make events happen through their internal motivation.

**Congenital disability:** a disability which is present from birth (opposed to 'acquired disability' arising from accident or illness).

**Co-regulation:** the supportive process between caring adults and children that fosters self-regulation development.

**Developmental pertinence:** practice that is matched to the individual's developmental rather than chronological age.

**Dyadic:** involving two people.

**Epigenetics:** the study of how behaviours and environment can cause changes that affect the way your genes work. Related term: epigenesis: how this process happens.

**Executive function:** the monitoring and self-regulation of thought and action to plan behaviour and to inhibit inappropriate responses.

**Experiential learning:** a theory proposed by the American educationalist David Kolb that children learn best when actively engaging in learning through experiencing and doing.

**Froebelian approach:** Karl Friedrich Froebel, German pedagogue, believed nature and outdoor play are fundamental to young children's learning and used movement, song, rhythm, and rhyme to provide key learning experiences.

**Fundamentals of Communication:** the social communication and emotional learning that underpins all other learning.

**Intersubjectivity:** the interchange of thoughts and feelings, both conscious and unconscious, between two persons or 'subjects', as facilitated by empathy. The term was originally coined by the German philosopher Edmund Husserl.

**Neural plasticity/Neuroplasticity:** the brain's ability to create and reorganise synaptic connections, especially in response to repeated learning or experience (or following injury).

**Neurotypical:** an abbreviation of neurologically typical, widely used in the autistic community as a label for non-autistic people.

**Pedagogy:** describes the application of the theory and practice of learning.

**Phatic communication:** commonly referred to as small talk. It describes exchanges through which people share feelings or establish a mood of sociability rather than communicating information such as wants or needs. Coined by the Polish anthropologist Bronisław Malinowski.

**Play paradigms:** models, very clear and typical or standard examples of play.

**Pragmatic Organisation Dynamic Display (PODD):** communication books first developed in Australia by Gayle Porter, designed to support autonomous communication and immersion in language modelling.

**Scaffolding:** a process by which adults support and guide students' learning, enabling them to reach the next level of ability, beyond their own personal capabilities at that time. The term was coined by the American psychologist Jerome Bruner, building on Vygotsky's work.

**Sensory dysregulation:** a state which can arise when the brain has difficulties with processing, modulating, integrating, and/or responding to information received through the senses.

**Social ecology:** the study of how individuals interact with and respond to the environment around them and how these interactions affect society and the environment as a whole.

**Window visits:** during the COVID-19 restrictions, families were permitted to see their loved ones in residential and nursing homes from outside the building through their window.

**Zone of Proximal Development:** the zone of the closest, realistic psychological development of learners that includes a wide range of their social, emotional, and cognitive psychological processes; coined by the Russian psychologist Lev Vygotsky.

# Index

academic 20, 30, 33, 61; *see also* learning
accountability 128, 156, 159
action research 11, 105–106
age appropriateness 7, 11, 54, 121–122
agency 89, 103, 106, 109
agenda: child-led 42; student's 104
annual review 136, 142–143, 148–149, 155
anxiety 24, 35, 42; reducing 57
arousal 35; high levels of 44, 80; pleasurable 64; *see also* regulation; sexual arousal
Arredondo, D. 16
assessment 50, 78, 87, 159; baseline 90; data 152; for learning 110; tools 87, 154, 158; *see also* engagement, Engagement Model; observation; Rochford Review; Recording Intensive Interaction Outcomes (RIIO)
attachment 24, 43; disorder 24
attainment framework 143–144
attention 22, 157; joint 91; shared 8–9, 17, 69–71, 109, 135–136; social 19, 44; span 20; *see also* concentration; fundamentals of communication (FoCs)
attunement 16, 24; importance of 43; *see also* fundamentals of communication (FoCs)
Augmented and Alternative Communication (AAC) 64, 66, 69, 76
autism spectrum disorder (ASD) 4, 77; and family relationships 153; impact upon communication 17, 19, 59, 76; importance of Intensive Interaction for 25, 29, 33, 57; and play 86, 88–89, 97, 102; and touch 117; and trauma 127
autonomy 8, 98, 105, 122; *see also* agency
availability 22, 81, 95, 145; emotional 128; staff 131–132, 135
awareness: of feelings 25; of others 43, 46, 49, 146; self 58; social 20

Barber, M. 154
behaviour: challenging 8; communicative exchanges of 57, 64; management 60; primate 115; repetitive 4, 97; sexualised 60; support plans 70, 132–133, 135; *see also* fundamentals of communication (FoCs)
behaviourism 5–7, 10, 87
body language 9, 10, 43, 56, 132; *see also* fundamentals of communication (FoCs)
Bruner, J. 100

case studies 21; autism and learning difficulties 69, 91–93, 94–96; cerebral palsy 46; EYFS 44; Global Developmental Delay 68; non-verbal 110; PMLD 67; video-recording 90, 97
child: centred 18, 32, 75–78; unique 43
child-led 42, 44–47, 51, 76; exchanges 23, 143; learning 104, 107, 109; play 87; targets 142
classroom: environment 46; Intensive Interaction friendly 54–55, 80, 90, 115–116; management 48; structure 107–109, 111

cognitive apprenticeship 34, 100–101, 104–105, 107–111
commitment culture 127
communication: complexity of 21, 23, 63, 66, 142–144; functional 20, 65, 70, 97, 149; phatic 20, 45, 58–59, 65–68, 115; symbolic 6–7, 89–90, 97, 100, 110; total 66–67, 133, 135–136; *see also* case studies; parent-infant interaction
complex communication needs 4, 32, 42, 44, 47, 118
concentration 17, 22–23, 45; *see also* fundamentals of communication (FoCs)
connection: facilitating 111; with family 153; finding 90, 97, 145; meaningful 29; need for 66, 126; social and emotional 7, 16, 31, 64–66, 70, 115; *see also* fundamentals of communication (FoCs)
constructionism 101
Continuing Professional Development (CPD) 132, 133, 145, 156; *see also* mentoring; training
control 42, 45, 65–66, 92, 120, 135; *see also* agency
coordinator: course 52, 63; role 78–79, 139, 147, 149, 154
co-regulation *see* regulation
curriculum 30–36, 84; broad and balanced 17–18, 30, 129; communication 66–67, 69–71; demands 18, 32, 65; early years 42–45, 51; focused 18, 30; hidden 30–31; mainstream 100, 105; natural 30; planning 25, 36, 89, 106–107, 140, 156; play-based 57; process-central 106–112

developmental: levels of communication 9, 90; milestones 50; pertinence 7, 18, 33, 76, 97, 117, 122; physical 32, 45–46; potential 36; reality 2, 6, 30–34, 37, 121; stages 9, 32, 87, 107, 144
directiveness 90; adult 32, 36, 87, 100, 104
documentation: best practice 70, 140, 147–148, 150, 163; school 80, 110, 134, 136; of touch 119–121; using video 83, 111; *see also* behaviour; Education, Health and Care Plan (EHC Plan)

early years foundation stage (EYFS): approach 8, 32, 81; development 32, 55–56; framework 32, 43; practice 47, 87; settings 42, 46; *see also* curriculum
Education, Health and Care Plan (EHC Plan): best practice 128–130, 135–136, 139–141, 147–150; tracking progress 18, 152, 155–156, 158; writing outcomes 142–145; writing provisions 144–145
emergent outcomes *see* outcomes
emotional: engagement 16, 43; intelligence 31, 38, 70; learning 24, 32, 43–44, 128–129, 153; resilience 32, 142; responses 114; support 137; well-being 17, 54, 60, 98, 116, 130–131; *see also* fundamentals of communication (FoCs); regulation
engagement: Engagement Model 144, 152, 156–159; level of 10, 43, 56, 97; social 20, 58–59, 65, 90, 100, 149
enjoyment *see* mutual pleasure

# Index

environment: enabling 42–43, 87, 105, 131–132; learning 35, 73–74, 80–82, 89–91, 97–98, 101–103, 112; nurturing 7–8, 29, 33, 114–115, 118–120, 131; physical 5–6, 81; responsive 32, 46, 63–66, 79, 83, 107–109; social 6, 66, 70; *see also* classroom
Ephraim, G. 9, 64
epigenesis 34
executive function 17, 35, 59
eye: contact 23, 112, 142–143; gaze 64, 67, 69; level 80; pointing 68, 70; *see also* fundamentals of communication (FoCs)

facial expressions 23, 64, 67, 69, 112, 158; *see also* fundamentals of communication (FoCs)
families: Children and Families Act 128; involving 25, 50; relationships with 58–61, 100, 120, 130–131, 153–154; working with parents 17, 53, 74–76, 84, 119, 128–129
Firth, G. 13
flow 9–10, 66, 68, 97; *see also* play
freedom 36, 97–98
friendship 20, 58–59, 61, 121; *see also* relationship
functional communication *see* communication
fundamentals of communication (FoCs) 9–10, 15, 18, 20–25, 29, 42–45, 90; FoCs 2 emotional learning 24, 43, 141–142; prerequisites of learning 22, 71, 90, 100; and verbal students 61; and well-being 130; *see also* case studies; Education, Health and Care Plan (EHC Plan); outcomes; Recording Intensive Interaction Outcomes (RIIO)

games *see* play
good practice 38, 55, 60, 159; course 133

Hewett, D. 16, 52, 75–78, 118–119
Hierarchy of Needs *see* Maslow, A.
hormones: cortisol 35; dopamine 16–17; oxytocin 115
human right 20, 90
hypersensitivity *see* sensory

Imray, P. 17, 100
inclusion 17, 32, 51, 70, 129
Individual Education Plan (IEP) 57, 135, 158
initiating 47, 57, 70; with peers 58, 60; *see also* fundamentals of communication (FoCs)
inspections *see* Ofsted
Intensive Interaction: philosophy 1, 51, 84; principles 23, 59, 119, 140, 143; without 60, 90, 129
Intensive Interaction Institute 3, 13, 129; courses 133
interaction: face-to-face 8, 48, 153
Irvine, C. 13

joining-in 20, 23, 35, 56, 64, 90–91, 97, 108, 128

Lacey, P. 78, 142
language: body 9–10, 22, 25, 43, 56; curse of 54, 57; delay 90; developing 45, 103; functional 20, 70, 149
learning: barriers to 16–17, 44, 66, 76, 129; error-free 23, 54; experiential 30, 34

Maslow, A. 24, 65–66
masturbation 120
mental health 15, 17; *see also* well-being
mentoring 55, 79, 145; parent 58–59; student 60
minimalism 57, 145
Moroza-James, S. 53
motivation 6, 35–36, 43, 65–67; intrinsic 36, 87
Mourière, A. 48
mutual pleasure 16, 57, 65–66, 115

National Autistic Society 127, 134
natural: approach 82; communication 9, 64, 68–70; curriculum 30; teaching 5
neural: connectivity 21, 33–34; plasticity 17, 34, 57
neurotypical 16, 100, 103–104, 122
Nind, M. 11–13, 121–122

objectives 36; *see also* outcomes; targets
observation 48, 69–70, 79, 83–84, 106–111, 154, 157–158; baseline 56–57; initial 90–96, 102–103
Ofsted 18, 48, 50, 128, 130–131, 152
outcomes: emergent 36–37, 106, 110–111, 151, 158–159; linking learning to FoCs 33, 155; *see also* Education, Health and Care Plan (EHC Plan); Recording Intensive Interaction Outcomes (RIIO)
oxytocin *see* hormones

parent-infant interaction 9–10, 16, 29, 64
parents *see* families; mentoring
pausing 45–50, 57–59, 92–96, 119, 141, 145; pause and wait 22–25, 47–49, 56, 68
pedagogy 31–33, 76, 101, 105, 116; pedagogue's role 73–74
personal space 20–22, 44–45
phatic *see* communication
physical: access 103; barriers 114, 118–122; needs 17–18, 24, 109; positioning 88, 118, 121–122
physical contact *see* touch
physiotherapy 45–46
play 8, 32, 35, 42–49, 56–60, 69; close sibling model 104, 107, 111; developing 102–104; free-flow 86, 88–89, 91–92, 94–95, 97–98; imitative 91; loose parts 87–89, 97; outdoor 81, 86–89, 97; repetitive 69, 87–88, 97; sensory 89–90
policies 119, 132–137, 148–149
positive behaviour support 132–136
process central 36–38, 100–101, 105–106, 140, 151–153, 159
processing time 17, 22, 25, 48, 56, 128, 136
profound and multiple learning disabilities (PMLD) 17, 45–47, 67–68, 109, 114–118
progress 18–20; and annual reviews 149; and the Attainment Framework 143–144; made in general 71; review 76; and the SEND Code of Practice 128–131; small steps 63; spiralling 37–38, 144; teachers' accountability 152; what it looks like 42–46, 50, 54, 61, 93–97, 110–112; *see also* recording; Recording Intensive Interaction Outcomes (RIIO)
prompt-dependent 22
puberty 59

# Index

reciprocity 115–116

recording: progress track 50; session sheets 49; video 90, 96–97, 109–112, 154

Recording Intensive Interaction Outcomes (RIIO) 155–159

reflective: practitioner 8–10, 18, 47–48

regulation 21, 25, 35, 57–60, 86, 134–136

relationship 20–21, 32–35, 64–66, 134, 153; cooperative 115; empathic 126; positive 43–44, 142; secure 97–98; trusting 45–46, 55–58, 71, 131

repertoire: activities 57–59, 71, 95; building 9, 143; learning opportunities 107; touch 120

repetition 9, 26, 33, 37, 107, 143–144, 149

respect 26, 76, 89, 97, 120–122, 126–127, 134

responses 22, 29, 67–68, 92; emotional 114; physical 158; responsiveness 9–10, 23, 33–35, 43–46, 83; tuned-in 16

reward systems *see* behaviourism

Rochford Review 17, 139, 153, 156–159

Rogoff, B. 34, 100–101, 104

safeguarding 1, 17, 116

scaffolding 29, 34–36, 69, 89–91; soft scaffold 101, 108

schema 87–89, 92–97, 102–105, 108–112

school: culture 131, 152; documentation 134–136, 140, 147–148

self-actualisation *see* Maslow, A.

self-esteem 24, 43, 164

self-regulation *see* regulation

SEND Code of Practice 17, 20, 30, 128–130, 139–143; *see also* Education, Health and Care Plan (EHC Plan)

senior leadership management team (SLMT) 53, 84, 126–137, 148, 152

sensory: channels 103; dysregulation 17; environments 108; hypersensitivity 120; impairments 117; modulation 81; overload 16–18, 24, 46; play 89–91; processing difficulties 44–45, 97, 137; profiles 76, 134; tactile defensive/ selective 120; touch system 114

session: finishing 26; skill-based 67–68, 87; spontaneous 25, 132

session sheets *see* recording

sexual arousal 60, 120–121

shared attention *see* attention

social communication: isolation 15–16, 32, 123; learning 16–25, 30–35, 60–61, 63–69; social constructivism 34–36; *see also* constructionism

social interaction 21–25; child-initiated 34; opportunities 103; priority learning 102, 149; *see also* communication; play

special interests 19, 23, 58–59, 87–88, 102

speech and language 7, 9, 149; delay 90–92; development 7, 45, 47, 57–58, 66, 103

spiky profile 32–33, 78

spontaneous: interaction 16, 34, 55, 82, 145, 154; participation 68

staff support 55, 145–149, 155

stress *see* arousal; hormones; trauma

style sheet 155

taking turns 23, 42, 57–58, 60, 69

targets: SCRUFFY 142; setting 20, 36, 48, 100–101, 144, 151–154; SMART 61, 142–143

techniques 45–46, 48–50, 93–96, 141, 145; pace 100, 140; positioning 22, 25, 48, 80–81, 95, 118; refining 104; tempo 22, 128; tuning-in 21, 37–38, 43–48, 64–66, 157

thinking: critically 43–44; *see also* cognitive apprenticeship

touch: avoidance 120; barriers 118–122; in classrooms 115–118, 121–122; consents 119–120; and human development 117–118; nurturing 114–118; social 114–115, 120–122; soothing 116; touchpoint 114, 116, 121; and vulnerability 118–119

toys: use of 46–47

training 83–84, 132, 145

trauma 16–18, 24–25, 126–127, 132–136

trust 20–21, 56, 66–68, 116

tuning-in *see* techniques

values: cultural 30–31; school 38, 53, 74–78, 126–134

video *see* recording

visual: impairment 44–45, 91–93, 120; supports 77; symbols 5–7, 66, 69–70, 136

vocalisation 23, 45–46, 57–58, 68–71, 90–91, 153

Vygotsky, L. *see* zone of proximal development (ZPD)

waiting *see* pausing

well-being: social and emotional 18, 24–25, 32, 43–44, 61, 116–122, 128–133

zone of proximal development (ZPD) 34–36, 78, 87, 89, 100–101, 104